Why Are So Many Relationships Failing?

Spiritual Bruises

BILLY BURNETTE

WESTBOW
PRESS
A DIVISION OF THOMAS NELSON

All Scripture quotations, unless otherwise indicated, are taken from The Amplified Bible, New Testament. Copyright © 1954, 1958, 1987, by The Lockman Foundation. Used by permission. Scripture verses marked NIV are from the New International Version of the Bible; those marked NASB are from the New American Standard Bible; and those marked NLT are from the New Living Translation.

WestBow Press books may be ordered through booksellers or by contacting:

WestBow Press
A Division of Thomas Nelson
1663 Liberty Drive
Bloomington, IN 47403
www.westbowpress.com
1-(866) 928-1240

ISBN: 978-1-4497-0900-6 (sc)
ISBN: 978-1-4497-0901-3 (dj)
ISBN: 978-1-4497-0899-3 (e)

Library of Congress Control Number: 2010941202

Printed in the United States of America

WestBow Press rev. date: 11/19/2010

Contents

Introduction

During the early years of my life, I could never put the pieces of a puzzle together to make relationships with members of the opposite sex work. We always grew further apart rather than closer together. Of course, I always thought it was their fault the relationships were failing. I believed if I worked hard and provided nice homes with all the trappings then I was a good father and husband. My wives just didn't appreciate me. I did everything I saw my daddy doing except I wasn't staying in a failed relationship.

I was too blind to see he failed in his relationships with my mother and us children. I was following in his footsteps, destroying my wives' and children's lives. I knew there had to be an answer, but I just kept trying and failing. I have four divorces and a eight years Federal Prison term to prove my failures. I even married one wife twice thinking I could put the puzzle together. I finally looked in a mirror, and it dawned on me, I was the problem.

During all my break ups with members of the opposite sex, I felt this great pain inside, like my insides were being torn out. I felt the pain physically, but finally realized it was a spiritual pain I was actually feeling. I learned to put band-aids and shields around those pains to protect myself from being hurt again. Little did I realize I was rejecting and bruising others through my defenses. I finally understood that for relationships to work those past spiritual bruises, all the way back to childhood, had to be healed. Band-aids only work for a short period of time and fail during really stressful times.

I needed to find a spiritual power that could heal my spiritual bruises, bruises that fed my misguided way of thinking. I had been to counselors and even tried churches that taught me a new way of life, but the spiritual power I needed was not there to heal my bruises. I needed a power that could heal the bruises- not tell me how to live with them. Until the bruises were healed I was like a sprinter trying to run in a race with a broken ankle. I just got frustrated, gave up and went back to doing what I'd always done before, only to fail again.

Growing up I was led to believe the spirit world didn't exist. Those who did believe in that foolishness were just unstable, ignorant people. After all we were educated people, went to church, had the Bible and that was all we needed. The church we attended taught and reinforced that belief.

But people who attend church are getting divorced at basically to the same rate as those who do not attend. How could they help me find what I was looking for with that track record? Wasn't Jesus' ministry about relationships, a relationship with Him that made relationships with others possible? Education and preaching didn't solve the spiritual mess I was in anymore than going to the secular counselors I tried. At least the counselors tried to help me learn some coping skills to deal with my bruises. There was a spiritual power out there I needed that would heal me so I could accept myself and others. I knew I had to find something or someone to help me with the deep spiritual problems in my life, the source of my broken relationships. I needed help from someone who was equipped to engage in the spiritual battle within me.

Before I went to prison in 1984, my eyes were beginning to open, and I started seeing that the spirit world really did exist and if I was ever going to have a relationship that was fulfilling, I had to learn more about the spiritual world and how it operated.

I have found the spiritual power I was seeking and that spiritual power actually does:

- Release us from the things that have us captive

- Delivers those who are oppressed [who are downtrodden, bruised, crushed, and broken down by calamity]

- Opens our eyes to see the truth about ourselves, others, events and circumstances through His eyes.

That spirit is the Holy Spirit of God, the spirit represented to us through Jesus Christ. Unless this power is operating through leaders and groups that claim to be Christian, they are misrepresenting the Jesus I have found.

Now, where there was pain there is life inside me to share with others. No more band-aids needed. I have now been married seventeen years and our relationship keeps getting sweeter and sweeter as the years go by.

It took me sixty-eight years to get where I am today. My hope is that you will learn from my failures and the success I have found and your journey will be much shorter. If I had just known, what a different life my family would have had.

Billy Burnette

Why Are So Many Relationships Failing?

Most of our relationships go something like this: you can see something good in the other person, but you can only catch glimpses (Genesis 1:31). It is like being in a jail cell next to each other; you reach through the bars to hold hands, maybe even to steal a kiss, but you cannot embrace that good person. Some go so far as to have sex without really embracing, like most married couples are doing today. How can we get out of our prison cells to be free and really embrace each other?

Only people who are truly free can embrace each other in order to love and be loved. This being said, we feel rejection from others and, whether they acknowledge it or not, we never realize they are experiencing the same feelings we are. Many of us do not know something is missing or know to hope for anything better than this kind of relationship, because honestly, very few people believe or know that something better exists. We have become comfortable living with rejection and are afraid to take a chance with real love. Most of us have taken that chance at least once, taken the risk on a relationship with someone special; however, too often one or the other gets hurt, feels frustrated, and walks away without trying to understand why this happens.

When this happens, it hurts so much that it feels like your insides are being torn out of your body. It is not the physical pain but the spiritual and emotional separation that hurts physically. At some point during our pain, we make up our minds, consciously or subconsciously, that no one will ever hurt us like that again. What fools we are! We want someone to love and embrace us, but we have no intention of letting him or her in, because we are afraid of being hurt again. Even if we want to give a new relationship a chance, we are constantly looking for signs of the pain that we once experienced to surface in order for us to justify drawing back behind our walls or lashing out to protect ourselves. We are actually the architects and builders of our own prison cells or walls; we are responsible for the barriers that try to protect us from being hurt or feeling the pain within.

We start building our prison cells early because of our selfish natures and our desire for self-preservation. Most of us try to have things our own way and wind up being rejected and bruised by others; while others try to satisfy their selfish and evil desires, they wind up seriously wounding us without a second thought. We build our walls or prison cells for what we think is our protection. Those walls do more than protect us from others; they are shields that protect us from the pain inside. If you are daring enough to think about the blows that caused your past pain, you can still feel that pain just like it was yesterday. As we grow older, our self-made prisons cocoon us, keeping the good inside our walls and the goodness in others outside, separate from us.

The more we try to be accepted and embraced, the more frustrating our process becomes. By trying so hard to protect our pain and bruises, we cannot see how we are bruising and hurting others.

Because we are blinded by our pain and hurt, spiritual and emotional isolation become a way of life, as does the constant bruising.

"What are spiritual bruises?" you ask. Spiritual bruises are just like physical bruises in the sense that both are caused by blows and result from something within us breaking. With a physical bruise, the blow causes blood vessels and tissue to burst, and the area hit turns visibly black and blue. Spiritual bruising causes something within us to break from the emotional blows we receive, but the black-and-blue bruise is hidden from sight. People see our spiritual bruises by our actions. When a person apologizes at the drop of a hat, you can bet something has happened to her as a child to cause severe bruising and that the child inside is begging not to be hurt again. The person with a chip on his shoulder is saying *you are not going to hurt me the way I have been hurt before; I will not let you.* This type of person usually winds up trying to hurt you first; he is just shielding himself within the walls he built long ago.

Naturally, our bodies send blood to our bruises to heal the hurt areas by re-absorbing the trapped blood cells that burst from the broken capillaries and tissues. Spiritual bruises are just as real, but they are under the surface and are not readily visible. As with physical bruises, we try to disguise spiritual bruises with makeup, hiding behind our walls and trying not to show our pain. Spiritual bruises can only be healed through spiritual blood, which truly frees us from pain and from the walls of our inner prisons.

When a bruised area is touched, we react in one of two ways: we back away and put up our shields or we lash out to keep others away from our wounds.

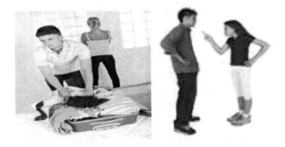

Spiritually, we react the same way. We put shields over our spiritual wounds, backing off to protect ourselves from anyone touching or seeing them, or we strike back at anyone who tries to see or touch our bruises. We justify

our actions by telling ourselves that others have hurt us before. From time to time, especially with those closest to us, those who touch and see our bruises learn to use that knowledge to manipulate us. We can be just as guilty of the same thing they are doing to us. Neither of us can see this, however, because we are all blinded somewhat to this kind of spiritual, emotional bruising.

This exchange of hurtful action is called pushing each other's buttons, and we do not realize the real danger it causes.

When we allow our children to see us pushing buttons, they learn at an early age that pushing buttons is a way of life. Not realizing the damage that has been caused to us as children, most of us get married, hoping to receive the unconditional love we have always desired. When the unconditional love is not there, both husband and wife tend to believe that having a child is their chance to be loved unconditionally. In fact, the cycle starts all over again. We want the unconditional love so much that we virtually put a joystick in our children's hands, and they learn to play us like a computer game.

The only way to receive the unconditional love we are all seeking is to change, and most of us do not like change. The reason we resist change is that we have to give up on our beliefs and our self-made protections and then have to trust in something or someone else. However, only we can

choose to allow Jesus access to our inner selves so He can change us. As we change, those around us will also change. Their buttons won't work anymore, and they will lose the control they once had.

When a button is pushed, we pull away, put up our shields, and/or strike out to defend ourselves. Either way, we end up hurting or causing others emotional pain. We are so emotionally blind that we cannot see that we are destroying others' lives out of our own fear and pain. It does not matter whether you use your shield or strike back; in either case, the other person winds up feeling rejected, unworthy, and, worst of all, unloved. When you think about it, reacting to each other through our bruises and pushing buttons is the reason all of our past relationships have failed. Unfortunately, if we don't seek healing for our spiritual bruises, our relationships continue to grow further apart. If we don't have the courage to seek healing for our spiritual and emotional bruises, not even for our children—who are typically hurt the most—then we should ask ourselves whether we really love our children or even ourselves. You would do anything for your child: buy her things, take her places, and give in to her even when you know you should not, just to avoid her rejecting you. So ask yourself, *Do I really love my child if I don't change?*

My parents never intended to bruise their children. Nor did I understand or see how I was bruising my children.

I was too focused on my feelings and myself. I did what I felt like I had to do to be successful in life, no matter how misguided my values were. My parents' misconceptions about what was right and important were passed on to my siblings and me. Because I did not know there was a different way of life possible, I have unfortunately passed these same misconceptions on to my children.

My daddy believed that if the man in the family worked hard, provided for his family, and tried to be a good man, he was successful and should be respected and appreciated. A few years before my daddy died, he admitted that he had been wrong to worship dollars and put money before love.

It didn't matter that he and my mother fussed every day and didn't get along, but it did matter that what was being passed on to their children was this misguided way of life. My mother believed that if she took care of the house and the children's physical needs, she was a good mother. Both parents did a great job at what they thought was right; we even went to church nearly every Sunday, which was expected of good, respectable people. We were raised to believe that as long as we were not like the bad people who got arrested, the alcoholics or drug addicts, we were a good family in the eyes of the community. Back then, that was all that really mattered.

Everyone liked my mother; she was a respected lady in our community and always received compliments on how nice she was. Many years later, I gained the courage to talk to my mother about how I felt about the fact that I knew she loved me because of all the good things she had done for me, yet I never really felt it. She began to explain to me that her mother was a businesswoman and rarely shared any affection. Her mother had died when my mother was just ten years old. My mother told me that her mother was not comfortable showing affection. My grandmother never intended to bruise my mother, and my mother never knew or intended to hurt her children or her husband. They were both clueless about what they were doing.

That day, after my mother and I had this discussion, I hugged her and she started crying, which was something she was not accustomed to doing. At the time, I was staying with my parents while I was out on bond, waiting to be sentenced for paying $50,000 to have a man killed who misappropriated a lot of money for an insider trading venture out of the Cayman Islands. Thank God he didn't get killed. My mother got up early every morning before I left, so that I could give her a hug. We enjoyed those embraces for the rest of her life. I look back on that conversation now and realize that my mother did not know how to show affection because she had never received affection herself. I am truly thankful that she knew that I loved her before she passed away and that she finally knew how to show the affection she had missed out on for so long.

My daddy grew up in a family that was cold, hard-hearted, and self-righteous as could be, except for my grandmother. My daddy's family was hurting. Their pain was so bad that their shields were made of the thickest, most impenetrable steel possible.

Desperately wanting and seeking that unconditional love, my daddy's parents would only allowed young children in because they felt these children could not hurt them. As long as they cared for and protected the children, they believed the unconditional love they longed for would come; unfortunately, it never did. In time, I was finally brave enough to hug my daddy, and we enjoyed those embraces the rest of his life.

My parents, like me, were successful in ways that hurt us in the long run. They didn't know they were just bringing on more pain by putting Band-Aids over their real problems. We all have believed we were winning battles when, all the while, we were inevitably losing the war. For some of us, it is not too late to realize what we missed out on in life because of our parents' and grandparents' misguided conceptions. This is why we have to realize before life passes us by that a different way of life is possible without the pain and bruises that rule over us.

As we all know, we live by example, and as life would have it, I became a mixture of my parents' examples. The one exception was that unlike my parents, I did not live emotionally separated from my spouse in a single house; I abandoned the house and looked for another relationship—again and again.

I became a workaholic, possessing the ability to have only superficial relationships. Thus, I ended up with four divorces, and I married one wife twice. I caused major bruises in these three women's lives, not to mention the lives of all the girlfriends in between.

Unfortunately, the people hurt most by my unstable relationships were my three sons: Will, who is thirty-seven; Caleb, who is thirty; and John Thomas, who is thirty-two. Out of all my sons, Caleb is the only one who married, and that just happened within the last year. My sons say that I got married enough for all of them. They haven't seen a good marriage modeled by their parents or grandparents, so why should they get married? The truth is the truth; there isn't much I can say about that. However, what I can do is let Jesus work through Cissy, my current wife of sixteen years, and me, and I can hope that my sons finally have an example that a good marriage is possible and that with Jesus, all things are possible.

I used the same excuses about my bad marriages as I did to reject Jesus. While Mother was saying, "Billy, you need to go to church," I was silently saying to myself, *I don't want any part of the God you find at your church; all I see is you and Daddy fussing and quarreling all the time.* Like Mother and Daddy, I didn't have a clue. I was trying to put together something that was designed to fail, but I kept trying and failing. If our marriages as Christians are not coming together in peace and love, we have no Jesus to share with others.

I basically spent my forties locked up after receiving a federal prison sentence that lasted more than eight years. I can now say that it was the best thing that ever happened to me. Few people get a chance to stop and look back on their lives and reflect on their mistakes, the pain they have caused others, and how worthless their idols have been. I want to share with you some of my experiences and lessons from those years and from the eighteen years since I was released.

If You Miss This, You Will Never Understand the Secret of a Relationship Full of Peace and Joy

Before you read this, write out an explanation of salvation that you would share with someone. Write a practical blueprint of what salvation in this world and in this life means in words a non-Christian could understand.

_____

_____

_____

Don't feel bad if you can't explain the process of salvation. Philippians 2:12 states, "Continue to work out your salvation with fear and trembling" (NIV). In Mark 8:34, Jesus says, "If anyone intends to come after Me, let him deny himself and take up his cross, and follow Me."

I accepted Christ more than twenty-seven years ago. I could not explain the process at the time or even to this day, and neither could the one hundred or more people that I asked, including those who were leaders of the church or longtime members. You might try asking your church leaders to do this.

What kind of foundation did we have to share with others?

Being born again happens as instantly as a woman becoming pregnant. And, just as a lot of growth takes place before a baby becomes a mature person, the same is true of salvation. However, healing is a process that takes place over a period of time. When we are born again, God begins the process of healing our broken hearts, releasing us from the things that have held us captive, and delivering us from being downtrodden, bruised, crushed, and broken down by calamity. Our new lives begin to grow and prosper. Our eyes are opened to see circumstances and other people through God's eyes (Luke 4:18).

As new babies in Christ, we should each be adopted by an older Christian who knows how to feed us milk and clean up behind us, just as parents change diapers without complaining and judging.

Adoption and discipling are God's structure for growing His kingdom. If we are not in His structure, we are not in His will. Outside of His will we will never become the person God intends us to be.

As we grow in Christ, we should develop as children do, growing toward maturity in order to help raise others. The process of being healed—salvation—can only take place when we come to Jesus and meet Him face-to-face. He alone can answer our questions as to why calamities happen in our lives. The older Christian who adopts you should lead you to hear from your heavenly father and brother.

There is a chapter later in this book explaining the possession of the Promised Land, which is a picture of salvation. Our freedom and peace are promised to us. We have to listen to God to possess that peace and joy and to share it with others. If we don't listen, trust, and obey—if we choose to be the generals of our lives rather than letting God lead—we will live defeated and discouraged lives.

If Jesus can't heal our broken hearts; release those who are captive from hurting themselves and others; deliver the oppressed who are downtrodden, bruised, crushed, and broken down by calamity; and open our eyes to see as He sees, He is a liar. If He is a liar, we need to burn our Bibles and give up all this foolishness called Christianity.

If Jesus *can* do all of these things, but we don't seek Him with all our hearts to get healed and to be made whole and we don't want to have peace and to love others, especially our family members, we are the liars when we say we love them.

If the manifestation of His power to do these things is not being displayed, and new baby Christians are not being adopted, the groups that call themselves Christians are misrepresenting Jesus and all He suffered and died for. What I have written is true, but it may be not as simple as it should be for people like me who struggle to understand these truths for years.

Everything in life is a bartering decision. Someone gives up something she has in order to get what she thinks is better for her. If you believe that what you have is better than what is offered, you will hold on to what you have. If you believe that you can control your life and have what you want, you are not going to give up what you have for something you do not know or trust. The big decision comes when you know what you have and whom you have failed. When you are willing to give up on what you have and who you are and make a decision to accept God because you trust He has something better, you are ready to receive His grace. The fact that He gave you the right to choose Him is grace. You obtain His grace through faith. The Bible tells us, "But without faith it is impossible to please and be satisfactory to Him. For whoever would come near to God must [necessarily] believe that God exists and that He is the rewarder of those who earnestly and diligently seek Him [out]" (Hebrews 11:6).

Many of us just want temporary relief, and Jesus gives us that relief so that we will know Him. If we accept Him as just a spare tire, coming to Him only when we need Him, our relationship with Jesus is just a passing experience, not a new birth.

We may fool others, but we can't fool Jesus.

After you have made the ultimate barter decision, you are born again and need a mature Christian to adopt you so that the growth process can begin. As we continue to barter our worthless goods for something of real value, we give up our hurts and deceit and receive life and truth. If you are not continually bartering with Jesus, most likely you have not been born again. When we barter and are proud of what we receive, we want to tell everyone about it. That is our bait as fishers of men.

Another example of Christian growth is found in 2 Chronicles 7:14: "If My people who are called by My name, shall humble themselves, pray, seek, crave and require of necessity My face and turn from their wicked ways, then will I hear from heaven, forgive their sin, and heal their land." This promise applies to us as individuals. When we give up on ourselves, turn to God, and "seek, crave, and require of necessity His face," we will see Him and hear from Him. If we choose to obey Him, we will be healed of the roots of our wicked ways and will begin to become more like Him. Don't be deceived into believing you just have to talk to Him. Scripture says to seek His face. No one knows the real truth until he *listens* to Him. The power of the Holy Spirit will bring new life to the area of your life that you bring to Him. If you try to short-circuit the system, you will become frustrated and discouraged. We can't change ourselves; if we could, we would not need God.

Salvation is all about relationships: a relationship with God and a relationship with others. About our relationship with God, Jesus said, "You shall love the Lord God with all your heart, and with all your soul, and with all your strength, and with all your mind; and your neighbor as yourself" (Luke 10:27 NASB). Only as we are healed of our spiritual bruises by loving God can we actually *receive* and *love* our neighbors as ourselves. Then we can let others inside, past our masks and bruises. Remember that we invest in what we really have faith in. What are you investing your time and money in? Unless we truly desire the rewards Jesus offers as we barter with Him (giving up what we have for what He has), our relationships will continue to fail, and we will grow further apart from others.

Jesus Does Not Want Us to Be Shallow-water Fishermen

When I was growing up, we never dealt with serious issues in church or our family; we stayed in the shallow water. Jesus is not a shallow-water fisherman. He told His frustrated disciples, who had fished all night without catching anything in their nets, to put out in the deep water and lower their nets for a haul (Luke 5:4). Jesus wants to heal the deep bruises in our lives. If we want to become fishers of men, we must deal with the deep issues in our lives and prepare to help others with their deep issues. Building bigger buildings, making better music, hiring better speakers, and launching new youth or adult programs in our churches are not, by themselves, God's plan to catch people or build His kingdom. Those things can be done without Jesus through our own strength and resources. They may bring a crowd for a season, but the crowd will never represent God until the deep issues in their lives are dealt with and healed. Only then will the acceptable day of the Lord be profusely proclaimed (Luke 4:19).

This tree is a picture of all of us. The roots represent the truths or lies we believe about ourselves, others, and circumstances. The leaves and fruit on the tree represent what we are fed through our root system. Until the old roots in our lives are given new life through the cross (until we give up what we believe that is in contradiction with the Bible), accepting the truth from Jesus, our root system will never change, and our leaves and fruit will never change. Revelation 22:2 explains that the "leaves of the tree were for the healing and the restoration of the nations."

Our leaves and fruit are for healing, but, again, that healing system can never function correctly until our old roots die and are brought to new life. If the root system is not healed, the leaves and fruit only bring the opposite of healing, which is sickness. This same truth applies to our families, our communities, our state, and our nation.

When we look at a tree, we can see the leaves and trunk, but the roots are underground. It is the roots that absorb nourishment to feed the trunk, limbs, and branches, which, in turn, produce leaves and fruit. All of our actions, the fruit and the health of the fruit in our lives, are determined by our root system and what kind of nourishment it is receiving.

The root, in modern terms, is used to describe the name of a computer file. A file can contain a lot of information that relates to the initial file name. The file name is the root of all information in the file folder; our initial memories, good or bad, determine our file names in our lives. A memory can be a very deep pain or it can be something that seems good; these deceptive memories may produce fruit that looks good to others, even though the fruit is actually bad. We all share the fruit of our lives with everyone around us, good or bad, especially our families. We react and produce files (fruit) that represent our file names and what is in our files. When things happen in our lives similar to a given file name, we always go back to the file and think and respond according to what is in the file, the root.

Jesus wants us to bring the root to Him, seeking His face to bring truth and life to our files or fruit. If we choose to accept His truth and light, He will heal the root, which will then bring good fruit. We can't produce good fruit without going through this process. In biblical terms, this process is the death and resurrection of the roots in our lives. Here are some Scriptures that describe the process:

> I am the Vine; you are the branches. Whoever lives in Me and I in him bears much (abundant) fruit. However, apart from Me [cut off from vital union with Me] you can do nothing. (John 15:5)

> Therefore, my dear ones, as you have always obeyed [my suggestions], so now, not only [with the enthusiasm you would show] in my presence but much more because I am absent, *work out (cultivate, carry out to the goal, and fully complete) your own salvation* with reverence and awe and trembling (self-distrust, with serious caution, tenderness of conscience, watchfulness against temptation, timidly shrinking from whatever might offend God and discredit the name of Christ). (Philippians 2:12, emphasis added)

2 Chronicles 7:14 describes the process for getting rid of the bad roots in our lives.

> If My people, who are called by My name, shall humble themselves, pray, seek, crave, and *require of necessity My face* and turn from their wicked ways, then will I hear from heaven, forgive their sin, and heal their land. (emphasis added)

1 John 1:9 describes Jesus' promise to forgive and heal us if we confess our sins to Him freely.

> If we [freely] admit that we have sinned and confess our sins, He is faithful and just (true to His own nature and promises) and will *forgive our sins [dismiss our lawlessness] and [continuously] cleanse us from all unrighteousness* [everything not in conformity to His will in purpose, thought, and action].

We have to seek Jesus' face and accept responsibility for the ways we have hurt others out of our bruises and belief systems. We can seek His face in many ways. The truth that we need to get into our minds is that He died to heal our broken hearts, set us free from the things that have us captive, and deliver us from the pain and shame of things that have happened to us.

Behold, *I stand at the door and knock;* if anyone hears and listens to and heeds My voice and *opens the door,* I will come in to him and will eat with him, and he [will eat] with Me. (Revelation 3:20, emphasis added)

For *God did not send the Son into the world in order to judge* (to reject, to condemn, to pass sentence on) the world, but that the world might find salvation and *be made safe and sound through Him.* (John 3:17, emphasis added)

If you grasp these principles and put them into practice, you will be healed and set free:

1. Without a vital union with Jesus, we can only bear bad fruit (John 15:5).

2. In order to become like Christ, we must recognize that our salvation (healing) is a process (Philippians 2:12).

3. We have to seek and crave His face out of necessity (2 Chronicles 7:14).

4. We have to confess our sins; then He will clean us (1 John 1:9).

5. He is knocking at the door of all our bad roots (Revelation 3:20).

6. He doesn't want to condemn us; He wants to heal us (John 3:17).

Throughout this book, I illustrate the ways that others and I have been set free when Jesus personally showed His face and spoke to us. Here are some further examples to illustrate this process in others' lives and my own.

A couple of years ago, my wife Cissy was continually saying that I became angry at her in the same way that my daddy used to become angry at my mother. I finally stopped and had a little talk with Jesus about it. I realized that I liked this anger, because it was a shield I used to defend myself. As Jesus and I had this conversation, I realized I was not only hurting Cissy, but also many more, including my children. If I really loved Cissy and my children, I had to give my anger up. I finally realized that I wanted to do this. I called the Man I am accountable to and made an appointment with

Him. That night, in a dream, I was driving along when suddenly I noticed I was losing a lot of blood. I drove up to my maternal granddaddy, but my daddy's voice was the one speaking. He said, "We are losing a lot of blood; take us to the hospital." Then, someone was going to put a silver necklace with a heart on it around my mother's neck, but the heart was tarnished. I said, "Stop! We need to clean the tarnish off before putting it around her neck." I realized the next morning my anger was passed on to me through Mother's daddy and my daddy. When I woke up the next morning, all my anger was gone, and I have had a new, untarnished image of my wife and mother ever since.

I used to try to explain God's decisions to help others find or maintain faith in Him. Last year, God spoke to me and said, "I am a big boy. Why don't you let me answer my own questions? Most people are upset at me for something they believe I let happen or didn't make happen. You don't know how to answer them and bring lasting truth and healing. If they will open the door and let me in, I will answer their questions and heal their hurts."

Now when someone has a question for Jesus, I let Him answer. How can I explain why God didn't prevent someone from being molested or abandoned? I don't know why someone died. Jesus said, "I am at the door knocking. If they will just let me in, I will bring truth and healing." What a relief; it sure takes all the pressure off me.

Since God spoke to me about letting Him answer, I have prayed with many people. Every time, Jesus shows up. I don't have any idea about what He is going to do or say, but He always speaks truth and healing to the root problem. Following are some examples of how He does this.

When people are molested, most often they blame themselves because the demon in them tells them to do so. I just say, "I don't know whose fault it was. I was not there; Jesus was. If you will go back to the time it happened (that is, take it to the cross) and invite Jesus in, He will bring in truth that you can use, as He did when Satan came to Him after He had fasted for forty days. Satan told Him one thing and He spoke the truth back. Satan had to back off."

I don't know what Jesus may say in the future, but in every case so far, the victims of molestation have looked up and said, "It was not my fault."

I say, "How do you know?"

They say, "Jesus told me."

In May 2009, when I was in the emergency room with a stroke, I had a similar experience. Two women, one who came to do the paperwork and the other, the nurse, both received truth from Jesus and were set free from the pain of having been molested as children. It is very simple. Trust and obey.

Another example was when I met a woman in a church I visited out of town and told her that Jesus would heal her of anything she wanted to be healed of that morning. She was in her early sixties. She said she had been divorced and was deeply hurt.

"Well, let's take it to Jesus," I said. "He will bring truth and healing."

She said she had something else that was hurting her much more deeply. Her brother had been shot during a robbery, and she had sat on the hospital bed with him when he died. She said she was haunted daily, wondering whether he was in heaven or hell.

"Go back there and ask Jesus in," I said.

She cried profusely for about five minutes. Then she stated that she was afraid of what He might say.

"If you don't get healed, you will continue to pass on this fear to your children and grandchildren," I told her. "Jesus didn't promise to tell you what you wanted to know; He promised to bring you the truth that would heal you."

She went back and cried for about two minutes.

I said, "You have to open the door and let Him in."

"I am working on it," she said. "Leave me alone."

A few minutes later, a peace came over her; there were no more tears. I asked her what happened. She said that Jesus had come in and put His arm around her, saying, "Trust me," and then all of her pain went away.

I said, "Go back to that hospital bed and tell me what you feel."

When she went back, she said all that was there was peace and love. Going back is a test of whether the healing had actually taken place, and, of course, it had.

One man I prayed for in prison had been molested by an older woman when he was twelve and she was twenty-six. He said he had a good and beautiful wife, but his attraction was to older women and strippers. At the time he was molested, he had thought the molestation was a good thing because it had taught him how to be a man. He now realized he had a big problem. He went back to the molestation and invited Jesus in, he saw what happened through Jesus' eyes, and he said that right then, all his lust left him.

The next man I prayed for that night in prison had been molested by his mother; this happens much more than you think. He said that even at fifty-eight years old, he slept at his mother's house the night before he came to prison. He looked up while taking a shower at her house and saw her staring at him. He had never been married because he had let his mother destroy each of his relationships. When he invited Jesus in, he said it was like a giant eraser came into his mind and erased all the disturbing pictures and memories. He said that if he had known about this type of healing, he would not have gone to prison.

The man whom I most recently prayed for spoke up and said, "I was praying to Him, and this is the first time those evil thoughts have not invaded my prayers."

On another occasion, God led a sixty-year-old man back to a time when the man was ten years old. His daddy had left him at their barn to fill the watering troughs for their cows. He started playing with the horses instead of doing his chore, and when his daddy came back, he had still not filled the troughs for the cows. His daddy called him a "no-good son of a bitch" and some other things. His daddy told him to stay at the barn until the troughs were filled and then walk the three miles home in the dark, and his daddy told him that he had better not let anyone give him a ride. He said he had hated his daddy ever since that day.

I asked the man if he wanted to forgive his daddy. He said, "Hell no."

"If you don't, you will pass this anger on to your children and grandchildren," I said.

"Oh my God," he said. "I have said the same thing to my son." Then he repeated, "I can't forgive him."

I said, "If you could actually forgive him and get rid of the pain inside, then you wouldn't need Jesus."

The man went back to that day at the barn, and Jesus spoke to him. He said the man had been wrong all those years; his daddy really did love him and he really did love his daddy. The next time I saw him, the man said he never knew that kind of healing was available. He had been reading the Bible diligently for years and was a disciple of a man who knew the Bible but who didn't have a personal relationship with Jesus.

I could go on and on, but we don't have time now. All I can say is I don't think or hope Jesus will show up; I know it. He has shown up 100 percent of the time. Sometimes I get a little anxious and want to say something or offer advice to try to help someone; that is usually when Jesus shows up. Jesus is not a shallow-water fisherman, and He has no plans for us to be, either.

Just dealing with superficial issues is a death warrant in relationships. It also misrepresents Jesus. Jesus wants us to go deep—and He wants us to do so with Him.

Why Didn't God Just Create Us to Be Good in the First Place?

God created the earth and everything in it, including a man and woman, and He declared it all very good. The man and woman were to cultivate, protect, and watch over this magnificent creation. What happened? What went wrong?

We all know the story. Eve listened to Satan, Adam listened to Eve, and thus they chose to disobey God by doing the one thing He had told them not to do. Because of their choice to disobey, they became like gods and seized the ability to choose right and wrong for themselves.

It must have hurt God to give people choice, because He knew what inevitably might happen—we might make choices that would hurt us or hurt our relationships with Him. However, He also knew there was no other way for real love to exist or grow, except through choice.

Let me share an example with you. If you lived under a dictatorship, and your wife happened to catch the eye of the dictator, and he decided he wanted her, what could you do? You could die trying to stop him, and that is probably what would happen.

The dictator could force your wife to live in his palace and force her to do just about anything he wanted. If she'd really caught his eye, he could spend millions lavishing gifts on her.

However, the one thing he could not force her to do would be to love him. Unless and until she decided to love him, their relationship would be very empty.

God knew this, and He knew He had to give us a choice. We can choose to love, trust, and obey Him, or we can choose to be our own gods, like

Adam and Eve. However, when we choose Him who first loved us, He puts the Spirit of His Son in us, enabling us to become what He created us to be: very good. It is our choice. Real love only comes through choice!

I Could Not Change Myself: The Meaning of Salvation

I learned through my experiences that I couldn't change myself or anyone else. I could change some habits to ones that were more acceptable, but the old me would still be there, unchanged and trying to make things work—only to fail again.

The word salvation means to be made whole, to become like Jesus while we are still on earth. However, I had a misconception about Jesus and salvation. I thought when I was saved, I was headed to heaven, and it was up to me to live a good life on earth until I died. I had not paid much attention to what the preachers said in church, but I did listen at funerals. I was led to believe that if old Joe or Mary did some good deeds on earth, like the preacher explained, they would meet Jesus in heaven, and one day we would see them again. I had done some good things, even better than most, so I figured that I should be headed to heaven as well. After all, I was responsible for building more than one hundred houses for low-income families. This logic—that salvation is based on good deeds and that it comes later—made sense to me at the time because the preacher was talking a lot more seriously about eternity at funerals than in other settings.

No one ever went to hell that I heard about, so why should I worry about going there?

Luke 4:18–19 says that Jesus was sent to earth "to preach the good news (the Gospel) to the poor; to announce release to the captives and recovery of sight to the blind, to send forth as delivered those who are oppressed [who are downtrodden, bruised, crushed, and broken down by calamity],"

and "to proclaim the accepted and acceptable year of the Lord [the day when salvation and the free favors of God profusely abound]."

The defining difference between religion and Christianity is that religion tells us how to live with our bruises and to change ourselves, while Christianity heals us of our bruises. Jesus heals us so we can really live, be free, and share peace and security with others. *Preaching and teaching without His healing power misrepresents Jesus.* Jesus not only wants to heal our bruises for eternity, He died so we could be healed while still living on earth. Without our bruises being healed, it is impossible for His light to shine through us. That is why the new covenant documented in the New Testament, Jesus' death and resurrection, is focused on inner healing. *Salvation is for now,* and if we receive His healing on earth, we will spend eternity with Him in heaven. I know this to be true because of all the supernatural healing His blood has done in me, through me, and for others.

My family's church taught that we were baptized into the family of Christ when we were babies. Then, as we got older, if we attended a confirmation class and went through all the motions, we had our tickets to heaven. Most people had gone through that process, so there was no need to worry about others' salvation. Hell was rarely mentioned, so what did we need to be saved from? My parents whole-heartedly subscribed to this belief. Similarly, my Baptist friends thought if they repeated some words and were baptized (dunked under the water), they were headed to heaven.

Like many churchgoing people, we thought we had nothing else to worry about. We were taught that once you are saved, you are saved forever. That is most likely the truth if one really accepts Jesus as Lord and Savior in his heart and life. Most of us didn't have an inkling as to what being a Christian was truly all about. Time would tell whether we were born again or not, which certainly isn't based on some one-time experience. Salvation does not come from a date with Jesus; it comes from a marriage.

It is awfully frustrating to try to change ourselves and keep failing. The effects tear relationships apart.

There Is a Lot More to Salvation than Grace

We have also been led to believe that we are saved by God's grace alone. Ephesians 2:8 says, "For it is by *free grace* (God's unmerited favor) that you are saved (delivered from judgment and made partakers of Christ's salvation) *through [your] faith*" (emphasis added). The *grace* is there for everyone who will receive it *through faith*. By His grace He loves us. Through faith we choose to love Him.

In John 14:23, the Bible says, "Jesus answered, If a person [really] loves Me, he will keep My word [obey My teaching]; and My Father will love him, and We will come to him and make Our home (abode, special dwelling place) with him."

A good way to tell whether someone has faith in God is to look at the way she invests her time and money. We tend to invest in everything we believe in.

Some people believe that attending church services and giving money to church organizations represents their faith in God. It is much easier to have faith in a church organization than to have faith in Jesus Christ. Far too few church organizations have requirements past attendance and contributions. The faith you have in Jesus is demonstrated by what you do after you leave your church building on Sunday mornings and Wednesday nights.

Ephesians 2:10 says, "For we are His workmanship, created in Christ Jesus for good works, which God prepared beforehand, that we should walk in them" (ESV). Walking with Jesus and doing the work planned for us is not the same as simply attending church meetings. The faith represented by a group may not be the kind of faith Jesus intends for us. The measure of a person's faith will be displayed in the way he lives his life. To illustrate, Matthew 13:8 says, "As for what was sown on good soil, this is he who hears the Word and grasps and comprehends it; he indeed bears fruit and yields in one case a hundred times as much as was sown, in another sixty times as much, and in another thirty." Fruit attracts people to Jesus, and that fruit will bring others into His kingdom. That is a true test of faith: a generous crop of souls. Why should a person attend church meetings if she doesn't have the faith to walk with Jesus and do the work He has prepared for her?

At first glance, institutional giving seems like a good thing to do. The sermons that say "bring the tithe into the storehouse" sound very convincing and proper. Truthfully, the real question should be, "What exactly is the group storing up?" Is it a harvest of new people dedicated to Christ, working with Him and gathering more of the harvest, or is it just the church organization? In fact, you may not be giving your tithe to Christ, but instead to an institution claiming to represent Him. God is not pleased with that kind of giving of one's time and money, and He does not reward it. He says that people who are not gathering with Him "scatter." Those who scatter are against God (Matthew 12:30). It is God's money and time; you should ask Him how to support His kingdom that produces gathers not scatters.

Questions for Thought

If you have a personal relationship with God, will you meet with Him regularly?

Is it possible to have a personal relationship with Jesus and not hear Him tell you to reach out to the lost?

In Luke 5, there were a group of fishermen who were frustrated about not catching any fish. Jesus told them where to fish, and they loaded the boat. If you are frustrated about not catching people for Him, do you think He will tell you where to go and be successful? If you are not going, it is for one of two reasons: either you do not have a personal relationship with Him or you don't trust Him. No relationship, no faith. No fishing, no faith.

God loves all of us, no matter what we have done or what we are doing. That is grace. We have to love God back for our relationship with Him to be complete. As we love Him, get to know Him and learn to trust Him.

There was a time when I didn't understand that if I was not gathering with God and if I was not on His side, I was not only running people away from God, I was running them away from me also. I wanted the grace, but I was not willing to offer the true faith and love necessary to receive and enjoy that grace.

Ceremonies Are Not a Bad Thing, but They Could Easily Not Be the Real Thing

Ceremonies, such as wedding ceremonies, are not bad, but they only provide an outward picture of what should be taking place within the heart. If two individuals have a real commitment of love, then their marriage relationship will grow and last; if a real commitment isn't made, their marriage will wither up and die. I had to be willing to come to Jesus as a committed bride comes to her husband. I had to be willing to leave the past relationships with Mother, Daddy, and others behind me, and I had to let go of my selfish habit of doing things my way. I had to listen to Jesus and trust in Him to help me knock down the internal prison walls that separate me from Him and others.

We may fool others about our motives and commitment, but we can't fool Jesus.

I repeated the marriage vows four times and fooled those women, who, in turn, fooled me when we repeated words without the necessary commitment.

Time proved that those commitments were not real, of course. I thought our wedding ceremonies would bring us together. I didn't realize the work had just begun. Those marriage relationships failed because we were not really committed to God or each other.

Jesus' desire for genuine commitment makes perfect sense; would you actually want to marry someone, knowing he had not truly committed himself to you? Jesus will not accept a half-hearted commitment, and until my commitment to Him was real, I would not be born again or become a real member of His kingdom. My true commitment to Him took place on November 25, 1983. That day was also my birthday, so it is a date I will never forget.

The Story of the Israelites

Receiving grace without having faith will lead to slavery and bondage. Using the story of the Israelites' journey in the books of Exodus and Joshua, God gives us a vivid picture of how we can choose to live in freedom or in bondage. The Israelites were slaves in Egypt because they had turned from God. They wanted to be free. God not only wanted them to be free, but He also wanted to bless them. All they had to do was trust in Him.

By grace, God sent Moses to lead the Israelites out of slavery through the desert to the Promised Land. Throughout multiple confrontations with Pharaoh and a manifestation of Satan (who, by the way, still has us in bondage today), God performed endless miracles through Moses. Finally, Pharaoh decided Moses' God was too strong for him. After losing his firstborn son and all his people's firstborn sons and cattle, the Pharaoh's losses were too great. He allowed the approximately 6 million Israelites, whom he considered his slaves, to leave.

On the Israelites' journey out of Egypt, God opened the Red Sea for them to pass through.

God performed miracle after miracle, and He gave the law, the Ten Commandments, to the Israelites. They discovered that they could not follow these laws by themselves and that they needed a savior to deliver them from the consequences of breaking the Commandments.

After three years, God led them to the Promised Land. The people sent twelve spies to bring back reports of what was in the land. All twelve spies came back and said the land is just like God had said it would be, flowing with milk and honey.

They also brought back grapes from the land.

The spies reported that there were also giants that fortified cities over there and made us look like grasshoppers.

Then two of the spies, Joshua and Caleb, said, "Let us go at once and take this land God has promised us." The people instead listened to the ten who complained about God and Moses and wanted to appoint another leader who would lead them back to Egypt and slavery. Their wishing to go back is a lot like so many of us claiming that we would rather live in slavery than trust God to face the giants and strongholds in our lives and be freed to enjoy the peace and joy He has for us.

God became angry that the Israelites did not trust Him to give them victory over the giants so that they could enjoy the land flowing with milk and honey. God said that those who were twenty years and older would never enter His rest. If everyone twenty years and older at that time never entered His rest, where are they today, heaven or hell? (Hebrews 3)

After thirty-seven years, all those who were twenty years and older died; then, the next generation, which was led by Joshua, listened to God. The names Joshua and Jesus are the same in Hebrew, meaning "the Lord saves" or "the Lord gives victory." Joshua was not alone; he had Caleb, a man full of faith, with him.

The story of the Israelites is the story of us all. We are slaves to our master, Satan. By God's grace, He sent His Son, Jesus, to die for our failures under the law and to pay our penalties for breaking the law. Jesus gives us the opportunity to be free if we trust Him to help us face the giants in our lives; then and only then can we enjoy and share with others in the Promised Land and in His rest. Jesus heals the broken-hearted, releasing us from captivity, restoring our sight to see as He sees, and delivering us from our oppression. We have a choice, just as the Israelites had, to trust God and face the giants or to never enter the Promised Land and His rest. Who are you following? Leaders like Joshua and Caleb, or the ten spies who were afraid of the giants and fortified cities?

In my previous four marriages, my wives and I tried to make our marriages work on the wrong side of the Jordan. We never addressed the giants or trusted God to help us conquer them and so could never gain the milk and honey (peace and joy) that God had in mind for our children and for us.

I Thought I Could Stake My Eternal Destination on What the Preachers Said at Funerals

Funerals are where the rubber meets the road. For some reason, it used to seem to me at funerals that the deceased always went to heaven. If old Joe or Mary did some good deeds on earth, like the preacher explained, then they would meet Jesus in heaven, and one day we would see them again. I had done some good things just like old Joe or Mary, so I felt confident about my final destination.

I then read the Bible, and my eyes were opened and I saw and an entirely different picture. God said in the Bible that only a few would find the road to life. If that is true, then only a few are going to heaven, and a great number of the population will go to hell. We will all meet Jesus one day, just as the preachers say, and then we will be sent to our eternal destinations. The members of the much larger group that goes to hell will see each other there and the very few that go to heaven will see each other, as well. Matthew 7:13–14 says, "Enter through the narrow gate. For wide is the gate and broad is the road that leads to destruction, and many enter through it.

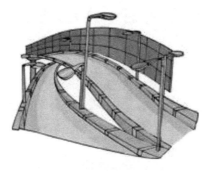

"But small is the gate and narrow the road that leads to life and only a few find it."

Luke 16:19–31 tells the story of Lazarus and the rich man. Lazarus went to heaven, and the rich man went to hell. The rich man could see Lazarus, but Lazarus could not see him. I certainly don't want to see the people in hell. If *you* do, you will have to go to hell with the rich man.

I learned the hard way that our relationships are headed for death and hell when we listen to others, even those we respect, without checking out the truth from God through the Bible.

Are you born again?

Your relationship with Jesus will answer the question as to whether you are born again or not.

Most people and denominations have their version of the requirements to be saved. We can take a few Scriptures and present convincing cases about eternal salvation. The Scriptures are true, and a person will do all the things presented in the Scriptures if they are really born again. It is easy to get misled into believing you are born again by those who don't understand the concept themselves. With new birth there will be changes in your spiritual appearance, just as a pregnant woman's appearance changes.

The Scriptures clearly indicate that Christ is the bridegroom. Those who have chosen to be His bride have united themselves with Him. Through that union, we are born again. Jesus said, "I assure you, most solemnly I tell you, that, unless a person is born again (anew, from above), he cannot ever see (know, be acquainted with, and experience) the kingdom of God" (John 3:29 Amplified).

The Bible uses physical examples to represent and explain spiritual truths throughout. There has to be an intimate relationship for new life to be created. A man and woman have to come together sexually for a child to be born. Jesus the bridegroom wants everyone to become His bride; that is His grace. A man and woman can go through a ceremony, but until they come together sexually, the marriage is not consummated. The bride has to agree to receive the male's seed. Jesus' seed is available to everyone; He will never force His seed (sperm) into anyone. It is up to a person to receive Jesus' seed with the cost and responsibilities, peace and joy that come with being the bride of Christ.

The parable of the sower makes a clear distinction between those who admire Jesus for a short time and those who receive His seed intimately. Some seed fell beside the road. Those are people who receive the word and do not understand it, a very short dating period. Some seed fell on rocky soil. This is a person who hears the word and immediately receives it with joy yet has no firm root, but is only temporary; a short dating period, no marriage. Some seed was sown among the thorns. This is the person who hears the word, and the worry of the world and the deceitfulness of wealth choke the word, and it becomes unfruitful, a deeper relationship; a longer dating period, no marriage. The seed sown on the good soil, this is the person who hears the word and understands it, who indeed bears fruit, some a hundredfold, some sixty, and some thirty; a marriage, intimate relationship, born again and reproducing children.

Another example of what it takes to have Jesus' seed planted (born again) in one are the stories of John the Baptist and Mary, the mother of Jesus.[1] John the Baptist's ministry of repentance preceded Jesus' arrival. A person has to truly repent (giving up on themselves) and be willing to make an about face, be willing to walk away from being god of their life and attempting to be god to others and over others. They need to acknowledge all the pain and suffering they have inflicted on themselves and others and then their sins are washed away. They become as virgin (clean) in God's eyes. Then they are prepared to receive Jesus' seed in them to be born again. Mary, the mother of Jesus, was more than a virgin. Mary knew what she was facing if she made that commitment to receive the seed of Jesus in her. She was engaged, a legal and binding commitment. During the engagement period, if she committed adultery, the penalty was death by stoning. If she was not stoned, she would be ostracized by friends and family. A person not only has to repent but accept a death warrant for their old self and be willing to be ostracized by friends and family. Mary said, "Behold the bondservant of the Lord; may it be done to me according to your word."[2] A person has to agree to open themselves up to become the bride of Christ

1 Luke 1:26–38 Amplified
2 Luke 1:38 Amplified

and receive Jesus' sperm, knowing the cost and the rewards that come with being born.[3] "For God so greatly loved and dearly prized the world that He [even] gave up His only begotten (unique) Son, so that whoever believes in (trust in, clings to, relies on Him) shall not perish (come to destruction, be lost) but have eternal (everlasting) life" (John 3:16 Amplified).

"And he who believes in (has faith in, clings to, relies on) the Son has (now possesses) eternal life. But whoever disobeys (is unbelieving toward, refuses to trust in, disregards, is not subject to) the son will never see (experience) life, but [instead] the wrath of God abides on him. [God's displeasure remains on him; His indignation hangs over him continually]" (John 3:36).

Jesus said, "For whoever is bent on saving his [temporal] life [his comfort and security here] shall lose it [eternal life]; and whoever loses his life [his comfort and security here] for My sake shall find it [life everlasting]." (Matthew 16:23).

Jesus said, "He who is not [definitely on my side] is against Me, and he who does not [definitely] gather with Me and for My side scatters" (Matthew 12:30).

Jesus said the harvest is plentiful and if one is not gathering they are scattering.[4] There is no gray area. Scatterers are running people away from Jesus, so they must be against Him, and it is very questionable whether they are born again. Can a person be a bride of Christ and not be gathering with Him? Can a bride of Christ be running people away from Him and breaking His heart?

Are you Christ's bride? The following questions will help you make that determination.

1. As a husband, would you feel loved by your bride, by the way you treat Jesus?

2. How much time do you spend with Him?

3. Do you know His voice and take His advice for you and your family?

---

3   Matthew 16:25, Hebrews 11:6 Amplified
4   Matthew 12:30

4. Do you brag about Him to others?

5. Are you committed to and bringing the lost into His family?

You alone will stand before Jesus on that final Judgment Day.

The most important thing is not whether you believe you were born again at some point in your life. The most important question is: what is your relationship with the bridegroom (Jesus) today? Are you madly in love with Him? Is that love being demonstrated daily? Praise God if you do have a great relationship with God. If you don't have that relationship, find someone who does and ask for help to develop your relationship. Jesus' plan for babies is to be adopted and discipled by older Christians. If you are a new baby, find someone who knows Jesus and ask them to adopt you. If you are an older Christian, adopt a baby Christian. That is God's structure, and if you are out of His structure, you are out of His will.

If your relationship with Jesus is lukewarm, you might consider reading Revelation 3:16, "So, because you are lukewarm and neither cold not hot, I will spew you out of My mouth!"

This is a time, like an annual physical exam, to seriously examine our relationship with Jesus, to determine whether you are born again.

Billy Burnette

Stepstohealingamerica.com

America will be healed one person at a time as we start living for Jesus and others, not for ourselves. President John Kennedy said, "Ask not what your country can do for you. Ask what you can do for your country." We are living in a time where we need to start asking not what Jesus can do for us, but what we can do for Jesus.

Inexpressible Joy During Trials

I am very hesitant to mention the below Scripture because I know what is on the horizon. Maybe my reason for being hesitant is that I am going through a big trial in my life right now, but I have peace and joy in the midst of the trial because Jesus and I are walking through it together. I know the good that is on the other side of this trial because we have been through so many trials before.

> [You] who are being guarded (garrisoned) by God's power through [your] faith [till you fully inherit that final] salvation that is ready to be revealed [for you] in the last time. [You should] be exceedingly glad on this account, though now for a little while you may be distressed by trials and suffer temptations, so that [the genuineness] of your faith may be tested, [your faith] which is infinitely more precious than the perishable gold which is tested and purified by fire. [This proving of your faith is intended] to redound to [your] praise and glory and honor when Jesus Christ (the Messiah, the Anointed One) is revealed. Without

having seen Him, you love Him; though you do not [even] now see Him, you believe in Him and exult and thrill with inexpressible and glorious (triumphant, heavenly) joy. (1 Peter 1:5–8)

In the past, when God told me to highlight a Scripture when reading the Bible, I would write the Scripture down on a piece of paper, and the Scripture's message would happen that day. I had "joy in trials" written down the day I read the above Scripture, and that is what happened. When I went to prison, the parole officer told me I would probably spend eighteen months in prison. I went to the first parole hearing, and they told me that I would actually serve 120 months. However, they don't make the final decision. That decision is made in Atlanta. So, when I heard about this longer sentence, I thought the parole board in Atlanta would correct it when they looked at the file.

We had periodic meetings with our dorm counselors and with the head of the dorm. It was on the day of one of those meeting that I had the 1 Peter Scripture written down. To my surprise, they told me that they had the final decision from the parole board: they had added 24 months, making my new sentence 144 months.

After the meeting, I went back to my bunk and couldn't stop laughing. I must have looked crazy to be laughing with such bad news. It had to be God. The dorm counselor thought I had lost it and ordered me to go to the psychology department immediately. The Scripture, 1 Peter 1:5–8, became real.

I could tell you many other stories about how this Scripture has become real in my life ever since I started walking with Jesus. I remember when I was on the run from the law, I kept listening to this song, "You'll Never

Walk Alone," on a tape I had bought. I remember the peace I had at a restaurant that Sunday morning in Hialeah, Florida, when I wrote my parents a letter on the back of a paper placemat. There is no way to have peace facing prison for forty years without God's help.

I told them I was going through a storm, but my head was high, and at the end of the storm, there was a golden sky. I knew I would never walk alone again.

I told them I was going to turn myself in. It was time to quit running from my problems and to start dealing with them. That peace was still with me when I turned myself in, and it was still with me on the day I walked into prison nine months later.

Trials are a lot easier when I am walking with Jesus and know what is going on beforehand. Like the day Daddy called me to tell me my mother was in serious trouble in the hospital in Tallahassee. I got in my truck, headed to Tallahassee, and said, "God, tell me what is going on."

He said, through that voice I have learned to recognize as Him, "Your mother is going to die in sixty days, and that is my will." I then knew it was her perfect time. She was going to be in His arms, and her suffering would be over. She died on the sixtieth day.

It sure is better to go through life not walking alone. We can have inexpressible joy during trials when we walk with Jesus. By the way, my older brother Johnny died the day before yesterday, and I have complete peace and joy. God showed me in a dream the night he died that my brother accepted Him that night. I had this dream before anyone told me that Johnny died.

Be Careful What You Pray
For Hell Is Real

Hell is real, and there are only a few people who are not going to spend eternity there. As Matthew 7:14 says, "But the gate is narrow (contracted by pressure) and the way is straightened and compressed that leads away to life, and few are those who find it."

Don't make the mistake I made. I prayed for God to show me what hell was like. The next Sunday, the chaplain preached on John the Baptist and how we needed to clean ourselves up in preparation for celebrating the birth of Christ. Christmas was just around the corner. After the sermon that day, I felt led to talk to the chaplain about cleaning up the chapel—and I didn't mean sweeping and wiping it down. The inmate orderly and his friends were watching sexual movies on the DVD player, for example, and there were other things happening there that had no business being in the chapel.

The orderly the chaplain had hired had been transferred to our prison for saving a warden's life from the Aryan Brotherhood. For those of you who have no idea about the Aryan Brotherhood, they are a white prison gang, and the initiation to this gang is to shed the blood of a guard. How were the African Americans supposed to feel comfortable in the chapel? This orderly was strutting around the recreation yard with his shirt off, showing the eagle tattoo on his chest, which signified his allegiance to and membership in a white supremacy gang.

When this man first arrived, I befriended him. He told me that there was a dark place in him that no one should ever try to disturb. He had already killed three inmates. He had cut the throat of one young man who was on the phone with his mother, for example; he picked up the phone and told her, "You should have sent the money for your son's drug bill."

On the Monday morning after I spoke with the chaplain about cleaning up the chapel, this man, the orderly, stopped me and told me I had gotten the chaplain in a lot of trouble for suggesting the chapel needed to be cleaned up. The next thing I knew, he grabbed me and said loudly enough for a hundred people to hear that he was going to stick me. I told him to do what he had to do. After the murder threat, I went back to my dorm. Not more than fifteen minutes later, the guards came to lock me up in a jail inside the prison.

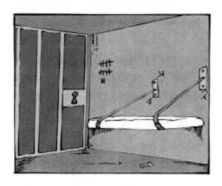

Solitary confinement is not a good place to be.

The prison policy is to lock up both parties after an altercation, no matter whose fault it is. Unfortunately, the chaplain blamed me for the incident when he talked to the warden. When the warden came to talk to me, he told me I would never set foot on the compound in Tallahassee again. He said I would be on the next bus to another facility in Lexington, Kentucky. While I was locked in that cell in solitary confinement for two weeks during the Christmas holidays, the Lord started speaking to me through that small voice. He said, "You think you are lonely now? This is nothing in comparison to hell."

Prison is hard, but the holidays are especially hard. On Christmas Eve, three inmates across the hall tried to commit suicide, all in one day. Hanging was the preferred method that day. Two tried with bed sheets and the other one with dental floss. The Lord told me that those men tried suicide because they had no hope, even though they had release dates from prison that were far off. There are no release dates from hell; the sentence is for eternity.

Adam blamed Eve; Eve blamed the serpent. Everybody in hell will blame each other for being there, and there will be a seed of truth in their accusations. The truth is that each person is responsible for his or her own actions. Imagine the shouting matches that will take place twenty-four/ seven for eternity.

God told me that it is better to be hot or cold than lukewarm. Are more people going to follow Jack the Ripper to hell or a lukewarm, nice person like a woman I knew named Diana? Diana never seemed to find her peace through Jesus. The week before she died, she took her fiancé, who was

Muslim, to see her personal mystic. More people are going to follow her to hell than an outright murderer. Just think of how it will be for a preacher who was a nice, charismatic person but who didn't really believe and trust in God enough to stand up to people. Then there are all the famous athletes, world leaders, and successful businesspeople who will actually suffer for their personal glory for eternity.

Imagine your child following you around in hell and having to see him being tortured day and night while having to hear him screaming and blaming you. Then imagine your grandchildren arriving, and then imagine your great-grandchildren.

There was a medical breakout in the Lexington prison facility, so that delayed my transfer. Several of the guards and high officials went to the warden and told him that the altercation was not my fault and that the chaplain was wrong. God speaks to His children about things before they happen. A friend of mine, who was an inmate, told several of the other Christian inmates about a vision he had in which he saw me walking back on the compound. That same morning was the day I was released from the jail inside the prison complex.

We have all made the decision to either follow Christ or sit on the fence in order to be accepted by others, trying to be nice and good in our own strength, or to reject Christ altogether. Jesus said that being good in order to be accepted is being lukewarm. You will lead more people to hell that way, and you will only increase your eternal torment. He would rather see us on one side of the fence or the other.

This experience reminded me that unless we make God the head of our relationships, we will experience a taste of hell regularly, with no hope of a parole date. Eventually, we will experience hell, the eternal separation.

I Didn't Need to Hear from God

I used to believe, before I really read Scripture or started walking with Jesus, that I didn't need to hear from God, but that He actually needed to hear from me and listen to my advice about how to manage His kingdom. However, in Matthew 11:29, Jesus said, "Take my yoke upon you *and learn of Me,* for I am gentle (meek) and humble (lowly) in heart, and you will find rest (relief and ease and refreshment and recreation and blessed quiet) for your souls" (emphasis added). I couldn't know Him until I walked with Him, and I couldn't walk with Him all the time without hearing and recognizing His voice. Walking and talking with Him is the road to finding rest, refreshment, recreation, and quiet for our souls. That is the formula for a relationship that will not fail.

In John 5:30, Jesus said, "I am able to do nothing from Myself [independently, on My own accord—but *only as I am taught by God and as I get His orders*]. *Even as I hear,* I judge [I decide as I am bidden to decide. As the *voice* comes to Me, so I give a decision] and My judgment is right (just, righteous), because I do not seek or consult My own will [I have no desire to do what is pleasing to Myself, My own aim, My own purpose] but only the will and pleasure of the Father Who sent Me" (emphasis added).

If Jesus needed to hear from His Father, how much more did I need to hear from Him to defeat the giants in my life, heal my bruises, and help with the healing of others? How can I be one of His sheep if I don't know His voice and follow Him? John 10:27 says, "The sheep that are My own hear and are listening to My voice; and I know them, and they follow Me." I knew I needed to hear from God, but I didn't know how.

When I was growing up, I didn't have to beg my daddy or the people for whom I worked to speak to me. They sought me out to give me instructions and their best advice.

So why wouldn't God, my heavenly Father, and Jesus, my brother, speak to me also? If they had an individual plan for me, I needed to know what it was. I knew that if I were doing all the talking without listening, then somehow I would be my boss, not God. I knew my will when I prayed, but I didn't know God's will. I knew it would just be a copout to say *your will be done*, because I used those words just to make my prayers sound holy. I believe God wanted to tell me His will; I just didn't know how, or maybe I wasn't willing, to listen. If I was not willing, I was saying that I thought I was smarter than God and that He needed to obey me.

The Scripture says that His sheep know His voice and follow Him. Jesus also said,

> I am able to do nothing from Myself [independently, of My own accord—but only as I am taught by God and as I get His orders]. Even as I hear, I judge [I decide as I am bidden to decide. As the voice comes to Me, so I give a decision], and My judgment is right (just, righteous), because I do not seek or consult My own will [I have no desire to do what is pleasing to Myself, My own aim, My own purpose] but only the will and pleasure of the Father who sent me. (John 5:30)

When Jesus died, the curtain to the Holy of Holies was torn open so I, and we, could have conversations with God twenty-four/seven (Mark 15:38, Luke 23:45). When I was born again, God the Father became my Father also. If Jesus needed to hear from Him, how much more do I need to hear from Him? I knew He wanted to talk to me and lead me, but I wasn't capable of knowing how to accomplish it. I didn't know anyone who actually had learned to listen to God's advice for understanding and instructions in prayer; to have a conversation. No one seemed to want to listen. Actually, we all were doing what we had been taught and seen leaders do. I am sure you have heard of the saying, "Monkey see, monkey do." Romans 8:26 says, "The [Holy Spirit] comes to our aid and bears us up in our weakness; for we do not know what prayer to offer nor how to offer it worthily as we ought." I had a problem, and I knew it.

Everything Jesus said was not written in the Old Testament. When He needed a donkey, He told His disciples where the donkey was and what to tell the people when they got there (Matthew 21:2). Jesus told Peter that he was to go to a certain place to speak to Cornelius and others (Acts 10). God spoke to Paul in dreams at night (Acts 16:9). I knew from these and similar Scriptures that God speaks to us in many ways besides the Bible. The words of the Bible are some written words of God; Jesus is **The Word** of God. (John 1:1). Without a relationship with **The Word** of God—Jesus—you can't understand the words in the Bible. I knew Jesus said that *my sheep know my voice and they follow me.* He gave the disciple instructions that are not in the Bible and I knew I needed a personal relationship with Him and I needed to hear form Him personally and through the Bible.

While in college, I had studied to be a CPA. I decided that I could apply similar study strategies and learn about God by reading different translations of the Bible and using Bible dictionaries and concordances. I could learn about God and earn an A in Christianity. I set out to please God, much like I did my parents when I made a good grade in school, even though the A's in colleges were few and far between. I could get to know *about* Him studying this way, but would I really get to know Him?

One day, in the midst of my studying, I was highlighting verse after verse, going from book to book. The thought came to me, *Who do you think told you to highlight that verse?* Well, I thought, *it was probably You, God.* Then the thought came to me, *Why don't you slow down and listen to me?* I knew that was Him speaking. I decided to put that thought to a test. Being an accountant, I drew up a chart. It had three sections across the top of the page and eight sections down the page, one section for each day of the week, plus a summary section. I knew from my studies that God speaks to us in three dominant ways: through the Bible, through a small voice, and through events in our lives. I wrote those three methods of communication in the three sections across the top of the page. I would read the Bible until I felt led to highlight a verse, and then I would write the message of that verse in the first column. Then I would close my eyes and write whatever thought came into my mind. I began to realize that the thought complemented the message from the Bible, but the thought was not in my words; rather, it was in the small voice I have grown to know to be God's. Then I would look for an event to happen that day to further explain the message. I would write the message from the Bible down on a piece of paper and carry it in my pocket to remind me of what I should be looking for. Once I started doing this, a confirming event happened every day for five years. Since I started this practice, I have never gone to a church service at which the heart of the preacher's message was not written on a piece of paper in my pocket from my morning time with God. I have learned to hear that small voice without my chart, but I still use the same principles now, more than twenty-five years later.

Example of the chart, but it covered a whole page

Day	**Bible**	**Small Voice**	**Event**
Mon.			
Tues.			
Wed.			
Thurs.			
Fri.			
Sat.			
Sun.			
Summary			

Jesus said, "Take my yoke upon you and learn of me"; He didn't just say to study. Of course, if I don't read and study the Bible, I really don't want God's advice in the first place. I want to continue being my own God, choosing right from wrong for myself, as Adam and Eve did. It would be easy to go to church and have the preacher tell me what God is saying. However, without knowing God, I wouldn't know whether what they were saying was from God or not. Going to church without studying the Bible is not the kind of relationship God wants to have with me or with any of His children. He desires to speak directly to us, just as a loving parent wants to talk to her children personally, every day.

God wants to speak to me, but I have learned that I first have to seek His face and listen to what He says if I believe in, love, and trust Him. We all invest our time and money in the things we believe and trust in. If I don't believe in, love, and trust Him, I will not spend time listening to Him or invest my time and money into His kingdom.

Here is an example of how the Bible and that small voice from the Holy Spirit work together. As I was journaling recently, the words came to be slow to speak and quick to listen. James 1:19 confirms that. Then 2 Corinthians 10:5 says, "[Inasmuch as we] refute arguments and theories and reasoning and every proud and lofty things that sets itself up against the [truth] knowledge of God; and we lead every thought and purpose away captive into the obedience of Christ (the messiah, the Anointed One). In other words, Billy, shut up and take the thought captive before you respond. John 5:30 says, "Even as I hear, I judge [I decide as I am bidden to decide. As the voice comes to Me, I give a decision]." I need to be quick to listen and slow to speak. I can do that, and it will be a good thing. I need to be quick to listen and slow to speak and do not speak until I hear that small voice inside me as the voice of God comes to me and say what I am told to say. I am struggling, but I am getting better every day. I just the made the mistake of speaking without listening to my wife. It is amazing when I listen and slow down to listen to the small voice what a more pleasant and wiser person I have become.

Don't forget that the Bible is our primary way of hearing from God. A person who doesn't read the Bible doesn't really want God's advice. You may wonder, doesn't Jesus live in us? Would a loving Father not talk to His children? A general doesn't have to listen to a private, but the private better listen to that general. If we don't have to hear from God when we pray, we are the generals of our lives and He is the private. That is an upside-down relationship with the one we profess to be our Lord and Savior.

In my previous relationships, in which both of us were trying to be generals of our lives and each other's, the relationships were doomed from the beginning.

God Knew the One He Wanted for My Wife All Along

My fourth wife divorced me while I was out on bond. Deep down, I felt that God would restore our relationship. One day, a friend and I were talking and he asked, "What are you going to do if she does not come back?" Honestly, being a new Christian, I did not know what to say in response. It was not by chance that I opened my Bible and began to read Hebrews 11:39–40, which tells of people who had faith yet did not receive what had been promised them. God had something better planned. I realized that if my wife did not come back, God had something better planned for me. I had nothing to complain about. How could I complain if He gave me someone better for me?

About a year after going to prison, I had a dream in which I saw a picture of my future wife and observed her personality. Five years before I met her, He told me her name: Beverly. I started writing this lady, and she told me that God had told her I was going to be her husband. The only problem was that after I slowed down to pray, I knew she was not the right one, so

I had to give up receiving her thick letters with perfume on them. It was really disappointing.

My roommate in prison had a daughter who was a precious and serious Christian woman. I was hoping she might be the one; again God said no.

Shortly after I heard this from God, the warden shipped me to a co-ed prison. I met a beautiful young Christian woman who was also an inmate. Having forgotten all about the name I was told, I thought for certain she was the one and that my belief *had* to be from God. The relationship was wonderful while it lasted. In the midst of it, I was sent back to an all-male prison. Unenthusiastically, I realized she didn't have the right name. After being released from prison, I did not date any women for nine months, from January to September. Of course, I had my eyes looking all the time.

Then, one September day, I told my preacher that I wouldn't be at church on Sunday because I was going to get my wife. Sure enough, I ended up meeting Cissy. We started dating, and once again, I forgot all about the name. One night while we were eating supper with a friend who had been in prison with me, my friend said, "You were wrong, and I was right," referring to the name thing. To his surprise and mine, Cissy said, "My real name is Beverly; everyone just calls me Cissy." I finally got it right. We have been married now for over sixteen years.

We both had experienced choosing our partners without God, and between us, we had experienced six divorces and left a trail of broken hearts in past partners, our children, and most likely, their children. Only God knows what is best; you will never know the best for yourself until you learn to listen to Him.

God, Are You Sure She Is the Right One?

After six months of dating, Cissy and I got married. Cissy had prayed, "God, I have messed up so many times in the past when picking men; if you want me to get married, you pick him out and send him to this church and have him pray with me." She had been divorced twice before. We both whole-heartedly believed that God had placed us together. It would seem, then, that with this divine matchmaking, of course, our marriage could be nothing but a bed of roses. Alas, all those bruises and walls we had sustained and built from past relationships started to surface after the honeymoon. Cissy describes the problem as "two selfish individuals coming together have to die to themselves in order to become one."

The same is true in our relationship with Jesus, except He has already died. For us to keep up our side of the relationship, we need to die to ourselves, too— with His help.

The difference between a godly relationship and an ungodly one is this: In a godly relationship, both parties reconcile themselves to God, looking at themselves first and coming closer together through resolving their problems. In an ungodly relationship, one party just tries to live with his differences and straighten out his partner without examining himself; ultimately, in this kind of relationship, both parties end up growing further apart. Each one learns to live in his or her own prison without trying to disturb the other, an improbable feat that only crescendos into fussing and fighting. Then, the isolation between both parties only increases, which leads to lives of loneliness and confusion. A commitment to God and each other is absolutely necessary. Without that commitment, no one can come together and last.

John the Baptist proclaimed Jesus as the Savior of the world. When John was on death row, John sent his disciples to inquire whether Jesus was truly the one or someone else was to come. Even as John the Baptist doubted, we will also doubt while going through struggles. Doubting is all too familiar for Cissy and me. During our roughest times, we each have asked Jesus, "Are you sure this person is the right one, or have we made a mistake?" Had it not been for our steadfast commitment to God, I guarantee we would not still be together today. I know that if this marriage can't work, I possess no Jesus to share with my children. The only thing I would be conveying to them, if this marriage ended, would be that Jesus is a failure and really is unable to build relationships that are rich and successful. After all, He died for all of us to become one.

Relationships are designed to fail when they do not include God. Relationships literally cannot fail if both parties earnestly seek God with all their hearts and minds.

It Was Hard for Me to Believe in Angels and Demons

I used to think that believing in the spirit world was for weirdoes. After all, I had been a CPA. What would people think of me? Well, I guess now that I'm a convicted felon, what have I really got to lose?

All the years I had spent in church and all the experiences I lived through before seriously accepting Christ didn't prepare me for my eyes being opened (Luke 4:18). The existence of the spirit world was completely foreign to me. Angels and demons were topics never discussed in my circles. In fact, my mother thought her son had gone crazy when I began sharing some of my experiences of the spirit world with her. However, I continued to share them with her, as well as with preachers and church members, all of whom thought I had lost my mind.

Jesus' kingdom is spiritual. How could I possibly function in a world I didn't understand?

Most of us have seen demons in action in our daily lives. We have seen people who change personalities after drinking. Alcohol is not the problem; the alcohol just causes people to lose control. Have you ever wondered what or who was taking control of a friend who had been drinking? It was a spirit within him, and that spirit doesn't display the character of Jesus; it is a demon.

Often in the news, we hear about someone who just loses it and spins out of control. What causes her to become so angry and vicious is a demonic spirit inside her. Nearly every one of us has demons, to some degree, inside us—even Christians. All of our actions stem from either the evil in us or the Jesus in us. Our biggest problem, for the most part, is that we are in love with the spirits that bring false pride, false security, or temporary carnal pleasures.

There are so many families, including mine, that have been utterly destroyed because of our inability to change or cause others to change. We only end up hurting each other. Living in a dysfunctional family bruises us so dramatically that our existing and future relationships are tainted. We try to reason with family members to quit hurting us, and when that fails, some of us blame ourselves for their behavior. To put it plainly, you can't reason with a demon. It takes spiritual understanding and spiritual power to seize control of the demon's power to dictate and manipulate. We need to know that we all can be free through Jesus' power.

In our church, we knew nothing about this power available through Jesus. We, as His representatives, should know about and be equipped to handle demons (Luke 10:17–18). As the Bible says, "For [although] they hold a form of piety (true religion), *they deny and reject and are strangers to the power of it* [their conduct belies the genuineness of their profession].

73

Avoid [*all*] such people [*turn away* from them]" (2 Timothy 3:5, emphasis added).

Many preachers and teachers adamantly emphasize the teaching that nothing evil can be cohabitant with Christ if He is within us. Going further, it is said that as Christians, our bodies are the temples *exclusively* of the Holy Spirit. Ask yourself when you next get upset or angry whether the emotion is swelling up inside you or outside. And is it true that someone with cancer or a terminal illness can't possibly be a Christian? Do the sick believe that their deadly diseases are extensions of the Holy Spirit? If you subscribe to this kind of belief system, then I have some oceanfront property in Arizona you might be interested in purchasing.

I am sure you are familiar with the phrase, "The Devil made me do it." The Devil can't make us do anything; God gave us free will. Demons were something I used to possess infinitesimal knowledge about; now I know demons will leave when someone who is part of His family and has His blood flowing through her uses His name. Be forewarned, though; this can be dangerous if you are not part of the family (Acts 19:16). Once the demonic roots and ungodly beliefs are exposed and the blood of Jesus is released through our words, the demon or demons must flee.

We are regrettably ignorant of the spiritual world. The Bible states repeatedly that people throughout time have wanted to take their gods into battle with them. When I was younger, I saw many movies in which African natives and Indians in this country put on war paint before going into battle. They painted themselves up to look like the demons, their gods. They had a greater understanding about the spirit world than most of us do.

We are doing the same thing today and don't recognize it. Do you know the name of the squadron that first bombed Iraq when the elder Bush was in office? The Warlocks! What kind of gods are our soldiers taking into battle? Parents are buying their children books and movies about unchristian characters, such as Harry Potter, and the children are reading about and learning how to cast spells. A lot of church members don't understand what is going on, and they do not believe in the spirit world. Many people who attend churches and claim to represent Christ don't even understand what happens to us spiritually when we have sex, as we become one with every one of our sexual partners.

Ephesians 6 states that there is a spiritual battle going on.

How can we be victorious in a battle we know so little about? I could share many spiritual encounters with you, but I'll limit it to just one. When someone on the prison staff believes an inmate is attempting to commit suicide, the inmate is kept in an observation room, strapped down to keep him from hurting himself. Other inmates are assigned to sit with him on shifts.

While I was sitting with a young man once, he continually rose up as far as he could and then fell back. He continued this repeatedly for what seemed to be hours, while I read the Bible and prayed in tongues. A door that was half glass and had a small opening separated us, so were able to talk. Suddenly, a demon came out of the man, through the opening, and went right for my head. The demon met his worst enemy, Jesus, in me and had to flee. The young man became still in seconds and asked if I would read the Bible to him. What had happened was real, regardless of whether

I liked it or not. Jesus died to set that man and many others free, and He empowered us to be part of the process.

It has not been as hard for me to acknowledge that angels are real. We know angels "are ministering spirits (servants) sent out in the service [of God for the assistance] of those who are to inherit salvation" (Hebrews 1:14). This verse is referring to those of us who are saved. Praise God that we are not in this battle alone. My mother's last words on earth to me were, "Billy, the demons just ruined our family, but we did not know."

Learning to understand the spirit world was an intellectual giant in my life that I needed to overcome. God positioned me to see this reality for myself and for others. When we are set free, love and peace begin to flourish in our lives. The real power is God's power. It is heartbreaking that an inferior power rules so many of our lives and our country.

If you don't understand the spirit world and how to wage war, your relationships will fail, as you will walk around blindfolded while trying to win your own battles. You will try to defeat your partner rather than the one controlling her.

Now I am a happy, spiritual Jesus freak in so many people's eyes, and proud of it! I am positive that taking this information to your spiritual leader would make for an interesting discussion and probably some enlightenment. Why don't you try it?

Demons Are Not Afraid of the Bible or of Someone Who Can Just Quote Scriptures

My friend Antonio and I once prayed for a doctor who had AIDS and was going to die. We prayed for him for about thirty minutes, and nothing happened. We felt that we were praying against a cement wall, though we prayed just as we had in the past. Antonio suggested we might need to fast and pray for a while and then attempt to pray again.

The first time I was prayed for, the person praying for me circled a Bible around my head. I thought I would try that, and Antonio agreed it was a good idea. I put the first chapter of Joshua in front of the doctor's head and quoted it to him. After I had done this, I told the demons, "You are afraid of the Bible."

The demons started laughing out loud; it sounded terrible. They said, "We are not afraid of the Bible. We were around when it was written and know it better than you do."

Although the demons were laughing, I could sense them quivering inside. I said, "You may not be afraid to the Bible, but you are afraid."

The ruling demon spoke through the doctor and said, "We are afraid because you *believe* the Bible."

Shortly after that, Antonio and I did what we should have done in the first place. We asked God what we should do. When the demons knew I was consulting God as to what we should do, the blood of Jesus started flowing through us and they became very afraid. Very few people know this, but you have to make spirit-to-spirit contact to have authority over demons. I then knew their names, because God gave them to me and I commanded them to leave. He was tested for AIDS several times after that, and there were no more signs of the disease.

At one time, pagan worship was allowed in the federal prison system chapels. The chaplain at each prison was instructed to have an altar built for the pagans to use. Several Christian friends who worked in the woodworking shop at my prison were assigned the task. They took a large reel, constructed the altar out of it, and then painted a pentagram on it. Then they took the top off the reel, placed a Bible opened to the Twenty-third Psalm inside, prayed over it, and then put the top back on.

That Saturday morning, as the men who put the Bible in the spool prayed, the pagans had their worship service around it. The worship leader exclaimed that there were strange spirits in the new altar. The prison system had these altars removed from all the chapels within a week.

There is definitely power in the Bible when someone who knows and believes it uses its words. Only then does God's blood, His Holy Spirit, flow through it.

The Bible is a love letter from Jesus and should not be worshipped or replace a personal relationship with Him. Demons have no fear of someone who can just quote the Bible or someone who is just a great Bible teacher and theologian. In fact, demons use the Bible more than any other written instrument to destroy the kingdom of God, as its words are twisted and watered down by people who don't walk with Jesus and really do not know Him. Some of the ones who fight the hardest and preach the longest that the Bible is perfect twist it the most by denying the power of Jesus in His children and the Holy Spirit's gifts for today. They want to feel important because they have read about Him and are eager to give their opinions on what the Bible says. The Bible has nothing to do with them (2 Timothy 3:5).

The Other Side Knows a Lot More about the Spiritual World than We Who Are Called Christians Do

How many of us churchgoers have been trained in spiritual warfare? How many of us know how the spirit world operates in our lives, our homes, and communities? Young people are turning to new age and other spiritual channels because they know the spiritual world is real, but most church groups don't deal with the spirit world because very few seminaries or Bible schools teach spiritual warfare.

They teach religion. Some go so far as to say that the Bible is perfect religion as it is; the power of God and the gifts of the Spirit, such as tongues, are not for today. These teachers say that we just need to become good little boys and girls in our own strength and follow the teachings of the Bible.

"Perfect" is Jesus, and the Word of God is not the Bible—it is Jesus. Scholars, scribes, and Pharisees have taken over many pulpits and seminary classrooms in place of the true men and women of God who know the power of walking with Him and the power of His resurrection. Most of those scholars have never cast a demon out of a person in their lives. I know I meet them all the time.

The Bible tells us some leaders, "For [although they hold a form of piety (true religion), they deny and reject and are strangers to the power of it [their conduct belies the genuineness of their profession]. Avoid [all] such people [turn away from them]."(2 Timothy 3:5).

During my last year in prison, at my mother's request I was transferred back to the Federal Correctional Institution (FCI) in Tallahassee. After I had been there a couple of months, an inmate came up to me and started sharing with me about his life. He was now a Christian, but very few in the Christian community wanted to have anything to do with him. He had been a satanic priest. I thought, *Thank you, Lord. You are going to use him to enlighten me about how the other side operates.* One of the first things the other inmate told me was that the only thing the satanic side fears is the *blood of Jesus.* He pointed out some ways that the satanic side was active on the compound and in the Christian community. For example, one of the inmates was teaching that Christians should separate themselves from those who are not Christians. Some of the inmates held a meeting in which they called me on the carpet for something I was doing wrong. They accused me of loving everyone and spending time with people who were not part of their sect or were non-Christians.

They also pointed out some things that I had said that were wrong. I have learned to listen to my critics, as they are not always wrong. I learned so much from the ex-satanic priest about spiritual warfare, including praying for your enemies. I started praying and listening to God, and not long after that, the head of the inmate group that called me on the carpet came up and said, "I can't fight you and God." The ex-satanic priest helped me pray, and the spirits that ruled over the prison were broken. The spirit of the whole prison changed, especially the spirit of the Christian community.

After I got out of prison, the Lord told me to pray over Madison County. I met with the pastor of the church I was attending, the one who took me in while I was out on bond and nurtured me until I went to prison. The spiritual high place in Madison County, the stronghold, was in the park in the center of town. Most people don't know or believe there are spiritual high places in every town, city, and state. We started to pray in the gazebo there. We walked around the town for seven days, praying and taking authority over the areas where we walked. On the seventh day, the angels of God came, and we could both see them because we were in the spirit. The pastor blew the horn, releasing them, and the angels defeated the enemy. I will never forget what the head angel in that army said as they were leaving. He said, "Don't forget about us when you pray again."

No one knew about our prayer but the two of us. The next time we went there to pray, we found a sheet with its four corners tied together, a dead burial wreath from the cemetery, a bar of soap, and a toy pistol. Over to the right was the same thing, but a Bible had replaced the toy gun. The police came, found these items, and reported to us that there had been some kind of satanic ritual done there. A story about it appeared in the local paper. The pastor and I did not say a word. A spiritual leader who knew a lot more about spiritual warfare than I did said the satanic side knew their ruling spirits had been defeated and they were trying to revive them. The satanic side was aware of what was happening in the spirit world and how their angels—demons—had been defeated by the angels of God. We all need to be aware of how the forces of evil are operating in the territory we live in. A word of warning: don't attempt to deal with territorial spirits if you have not dealt with spirits in people, and get prepared to fight in major battles.

Where are our watchmen? Does your church have a watchman who knows and sees what is spiritually going on in the church and town you live in? Do you know what is spiritually going on in your household? Trust me on this: the satanic side has a strategy, and the demons know what is going on and are about their business.

Do you and your group have a spiritual strategy? Are you involved in spiritual warfare, or are you and your leaders walking around with blinders on?

Is the enemy is overrunning our families and country? Maybe it is time to climb back in my tower. Everyone needs to have spiritual eyes to see what is going on around them spiritually. If you don't, you will shadow box and hurt people rather than the real enemy.

I Was Clueless about What Was Going On in a Sexually Disturbed Person's Mind

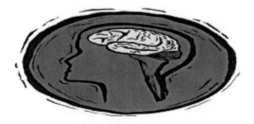

I have never met a sexual molester who has not been molested. There are two types of offenders: ones who love their sin and ones who fight it. Allow me to share with you two experiences. There was a man who, prior to being sent to prison, was a youth minister. He told me of instances in which a very highly regarded minister some years ago got caught in some pretty nasty sexual stuff, and now that minister could never be set free. I thought, *What in the world is he talking about?* He went on to say that he, like the minister, couldn't be set free for the same reason, because they were both in love with the sexual perversion they had committed. People with that train of thought have little to no hope of ever changing.

Let me share with you the story of another man who attended a Kairos retreat, a four-day ministry for prisoners. He obviously came from a wealthy family from West Palm Beach, and he had on an expensive pair of glasses.

He was very intellectual, having written and published three books since his incarceration.

I walked up to him and said, "You're going to have a difficult time with Christianity, because you are smart, but you are nowhere near as smart as God." I asked him what his problem was, not why he was in prison. He responded by stating that his wife of over twenty years was with another man just three weeks after he was taken into custody. Instantly, I replied that she probably had wanted to leave for a long time, but I inquired further as to what the real underlying problem was. He said there was a monster in him. I agreed with him that this was not a good thing, but I had dealt with monsters and could help him.

He began his story by saying that when he was young boy, his father had molested him.

He was sent to Catholic school, where the priest had sexually abused him as well.

He continued to tell me that for over thirty years, something inside him was trying to get him to commit these acts against someone else, but he refused to concede to those urges. With each passing year, the temptation grew, and the monster got stronger and stronger. He told me to imagine the strongest sexual desire you have ever felt and then multiply that by two. That is what he faced every day. I began to pray with him, and the demon came out through the power of the blood of Jesus. He said to me that *he never knew he could be set free,* and I will never forget those words.

Later that evening in the retreat center, where we volunteers were staying, the leader of the ministry asked if I would lead the Communion service. I politely declined, feeling that that was a preacher's job, not mine. My belief is that the bread symbolizes the words of God to us. We are supposed to take those words, ingest them into our spirits for nourishment, drink in God's love, and be servants of His kingdom. After I thought I had avoided a close call, the preacher asked me to serve the grape juice.

While holding that plastic cup of juice, I was going to repeat the expected words, "God's blood, shed for you," but in that instant, God spoke to me. He spoke gently within my heart; well, maybe not so gently.

"Billy, you really don't appreciate this stuff," He said. I tried to make an excuse, but He didn't go for it. "This is resurrected blood you are drinking, blood that has the power to set people free, like that man you prayed for this morning. Playing church will not appease me. If you're not going to do it right, do not come back up here to half-heartedly drink my resurrected blood."

My prayer now is that I never come in contact with anyone who will ever go away from me without knowing that he can be set free, and that I will always have the courage to help him receive that freedom. Can you imagine the frustration that goes on in couples' lives when they do not know that the answer—freedom—has been available all along, but they have never met anyone who could lead them to a relationship with Jesus.

Power Released When Christians Pray

When I accepted Christ in 1983, I came back home while out on bond, awaiting sentencing eight months later. My eyes were opened as to the power of prayer and the effect it had on my life. Many people prayed for me, and I thank God for their prayers. There was one special lady, Mrs. Blake, who really reached the throne room of God. It was her prayers that put the thought in my head to go to church that Sunday morning. That's when my eyes were opened to see Jesus in another person and accept Him as the Lord of my life. Mrs. Blake attended a denominational church that preached and taught against the power of the Spirit and the gifts of the Spirit for today. But believe me, she did not go for that foolishness. If you do, tear out the pages in the New Testament that speak of the power of God moving through people. Especially tear out John 14:12 (Amplified Bible) where Jesus said, "I assure you, most solemnly I tell you, if **anyone** steadfastly believes in Me, he will himself be able to do the things that I do; and he will do even greater things than these, because I go to the Father." In addition, tear out 2 Timothy 3:5 speaking of leaders. "For [although] they hold a form of piety (true religion), they deny and reject and are strangers to the power of it [their conduct belies the genuineness of their profession]. Avoid [all] such people [turn away from them]."

Without the power of God and the Holy Spirit moving in us and through us as it did in Jesus, there is no Christianity. After all, isn't His Spirit in us who believe?

Shortly after going to prison, I decided to slow down and have a talk with God about prayer. The main thing I learned from that conversation was that spiritual prayer is what keeps His heart beating in His body on earth. Without spiritual prayers, everything is done in the flesh. We know from Romans 14:23 AMP, "For whatever does not originate and proceed from faith is sin [whatever is done without conviction of its approval by God is sinful]."

In prison, when a Christian inmate would tell another inmate who was running from Christ that he was going to start praying for, the person would become very angry. He understood that the evil in him was going to be stirred up, and he was not going to get much sleep. If someone said they were going to fast for him, he would want to fight.

From time to time, the Holy Spirit leads me to someone who has gotten him- or herself into trouble. I say to them, "I'll tell you something about yourself." They look amazed and want to know what it is. I ask them, if two people are breaking into a building and one has a spotlight on them and the other one does not, which is the most likely to get caught? Of course, they always say the one with the spotlight on them. I explain that the prayers of their mother or grandmother (as the Lord leads) put a spotlight on you, and that is why you got caught. In fact, you got caught when others didn't. You also had to take drugs or drink alcohol to do the things you did, to be able to go along with the crowd; they agree. The sad part is that when they get caught, that same person who prayed is the first one to try to bail them out. Their prayers were answered, just not the way they expected. The praying person needs to step out of the way, let them face the consequences of their actions, and let them and God handle their problem. If you don't, the person will just get into more and bigger trouble; I know from my own experience.

As we grow in Christ, we will continually learn and become more effective in our prayer life. These are some things I've learned:

1. Prayer is a discussion with God. We make a request. He listens. We listen to what He tells us to say and do. When we say and do as instructed, the Holy Spirit moves through us with the power of heaven.

2. Sometimes it is better to sit down with a blank sheet of paper and just listen to hear what He wants to talk about.

3. We can hear His still, small voice through the Bible, through preaching and teaching, through others, and through dreams and visions. We just need to have a personal relationship, so we know He is speaking, in any way He chooses.

4. Sometimes when we pray, we will see good results; that's wonderful.

5. Sometimes bad things will start happening as a battle starts to rage. When that happens, if we are hearing from God, we will start praising Him. We know the battle is on and the victory is at hand. Then we need to continue to pray more earnestly.

6. This is especially true when praying for other people. If they're a drinker, they will start drinking more than ever. If they are on drugs, they will start using more drugs. If they're an angry person, they will become angrier. If God has led you to pray for that person, you are in a battle you can't lose unless you give up.

7. Pray for your enemies. The enemy is not the person, it is the spirit in them. Make sure you examine the plank in your eye before condemning them. It just might be the wrong spirit in you fighting against an evil spirit in them. If you keep praying and listening to God, both of you will change.

8. Pray in tongues. If you are a Christian, it will not be you praying but the Spirit in you, as the power of the blood of Jesus is released.

9. Sometimes a prayer is not completed until we do as instructed.

10. Prayer moves mountains.

Remember, if you are not doing much praying, your spiritual heart is not beating well and your sinful nature will be represented in nearly everything done in you and through you. God gave Joshua some good advice, and if we walk with God, He will be with us as He was with Joshua. Joshua 1:5 AMP says, "No man shall be able to stand before you all the days of your life. As I was with Moses, so I will be with you; I will not fail you or forsake you."

We can only lose if we fail to pray, crave out of necessity His face, trust and obey.

Why Would a Christian Not Want to Pray in Tongues?

There are two main reasons that a Christian may not want to pray in tongues:

1. We do not want to lose control. The tongue is a mighty muscle that we have used to control others, and we do not want to give that control to the Spirit of God (James 3:5–8).

2. We do not understand praying in tongues, what happens in us when we pray in tongues, or what the living water that leaves us accomplishes for God's kingdom in others.

This is what I understand about praying in tongues, from the Bible.

> We do not know what prayer to offer nor how to offer it worthily as we ought, but the Spirit Himself goes to meet our supplication and pleads in our behalf with unspeakable yearnings and groanings too deep for utterance. And He who searches the hearts of men knows what is in the mind of the [Holy] Spirit [what his intent is], because the Spirit intercedes and pleads [before God] in behalf of the saints according to and in harmony with God's will. (Romans 8:26–27)

> For who speaks in an [unknown] tongue speaks not to men but to God, for no one understands or catches his meaning, because in the [Holy Spirit], he utters secret truths and hidden things [not obvious to the understanding]. (1 Corinthians 14:2)

These two verses seem to be in agreement. We do not fully know what is going on in the situation we want to pray for; only God knows what is needed and how to bring His best.

We, particularly in the United States, have the hardest time accepting a king or lord over our lives because we live in a democracy and have the right to choose for ourselves.

What is good and evil? Adam and Eve chose to decide for themselves what was good and evil, and that choice got them a one-way ticket to eternal hell (Genesis 3). When we say the Pledge of Allegiance, we say "one nation under God," but it seems we have chosen, like Adam and Eve, to bypass God and be gods among ourselves.

One day as I was praying, the Lord asked me, "Billy, am I your Lord or your servant?"

I answered with the appropriate religious words, "You are my Lord and Master."

He replied, "I don't think so; listen to your prayers. A master doesn't have to hear from his servants; he defines for them what to do and how to do it. A servant must listen to the master to remain in his kingdom. Do you have to listen to me when you pray? No, you just ask me to do what you think is best for yourself and others. You act as the master, telling me what needs to be done, and, to sound holy, you toss in religious-sounding words you have heard others say, such as 'not my will, but Yours.'"

Jesus spoke those very words right before He went to the cross. He said, "Father, if You are willing, remove this cup from Me; yet not My will, but [always] Yours be done" (Luke 22:42).

The Lord continued to speak to me, saying, "When you pray, you don't know my will" (see Romans 8:26–27). "Don't you think I will tell you my will? Do you have to beg your boss to tell you what to do?

No, he wants to tell you what to do, and it is his responsibility to give you what you need to carry out his requests. If you treated your boss the way you treat me, how long would it take him to fire you? You have remained a baby and are copying those who claim to be grown up but are just babies themselves."

Can you imagine how God feels when someone who is a spiritual teen or adult keeps asking Him to do everything? The person sounds like a spoiled child.

He has given us the keys to the kingdom (Matthew 16:19). As we grow, we should begin to know and understand "the immeasurable, unlimited and surpassing greatness of His power in and for those of us who believe, as demonstrated in the working of His mighty strength which He exerted in Christ when He raised Him from the dead and seated Him at His [own] right hand in the heavenly [places], far above all rule and authority and power and dominion and every name that is named [above every title that can be conferred], not only in this age and in this world, but also in the age and the world which is to come" (Ephesians 1:19–21). When we became His children, He "raised us up together with Jesus and made us sit down together [giving us joint seating with Jesus] in the heavenly sphere [by virtue of our being] in Christ Jesus (the Messiah, the Anointed one)" (Ephesians 2:6).

Here we are, spiritually seated with Jesus, asking God to do this and that, when He has given us authority and power within ourselves to accomplish so much. If we would only listen and obey Him, as Jesus did, God's power would be exhibited through us. Our teachers are babies themselves, but we've believed them to be mature Christian leaders. Many leaders have not grown to become even a fraction of all that God wants them to be so that they might lead us to spiritual maturity. However, we can't possibly try to blame someone who was herself trained by babies and was herself discouraged from growing any further. Eventually, we all must get out of our comfort zones.

It is time for us to grow beyond the normal church mold of a "typical" Christian. We must develop into all God intends us to be, not what a church, preacher, or society wants us to be. We are filled with the Holy Spirit so that we may bring about salvation (freedom) for others and ourselves.

Praying in unknown tongues is one of the ways we reverse the situation and come into agreement with God and His wishes in a Lord/servant relationship. The Bible says, "We are assured and know that [*God being a partner in their labor*] all things work together and are [fitting into a plan] for good to and for those who love God and are called *according to [His] design and purpose*" (Romans 8:28, emphasis added). When we are aligned with His purpose, He serves with us, and the power of the Holy Spirit will be released through us. Praying in unknown tongues is a giant step in humility. It is good for us to submit to God, but not to ask Him to submit to us.

While I was out on bond, although facing a serious prison sentence, I accepted Christ. During that time, I heard about a friend I'd grown up with who had started speaking in tongues. I thought about it and said, "She has gone crazy." Having been raised in a Methodist church, I never heard anyone speak or teach about praying in tongues.

I had overheard my parents make jokes about the crazies who were involved in that sort of "emotional" Christianity. That kind of stuff was not for educated people like us.

Shortly after hearing about my friend, I attended a small independent church on the outskirts of town. This church took me in and wanted to help me spiritually.

The shallow religious activities of the Methodist church were not what I needed for the problems that faced me when I was awaiting my sentence. I was willing to do anything God had in store for me at that time. The small church that took me in had a guest speaker who asked if anyone wanted a miracle. I held up my hand along with everyone else. I did not want to go to prison. He said most of us already had the miracle we wanted, but were not prepared to receive it. He went on and drew a comparison to the receiver who caught the winning touchdown in the Super Bowl. The receiver didn't just walk on the field that day and decide to play in the Super Bowl. He had to work and practice long and hard to play in that game.

After I thought about it for a while, the miracles I really wanted were to have a successful marriage, to be accepted as I was, and then to pass that peace on to my children. I had been through four divorces and was never prepared for those marriages in the first place. I knew I could easily go back to my ex-wife, but I also knew I was not prepared to carry the marriage across the goal line.

A night or two later, this same guest speaker asked if any of us wanted to receive a prayer language that would help us prepare to receive our miracle. I moved hastily to the altar. That night I received just a few syllables, but I knew they were from God. There was a couple there with whom I had attended school nearly my whole life. They also received their prayer language. They said they had been preparing for years to receive it. I have now learned that you don't need to get ready to receive a gift that prepares you for your miracle. God wants to give us all the tools we need as rapidly as we will accept them.

During the time I was out on bond, I had to drive thirty miles each weekday to report to my parole officer. During my daily drive, I struggled just to get the words out in this new language. It was extremely difficult for me to give up control of my tongue to a spirit; I had had control over it for so long, all the while controlling others. When trying to let go and allow the spirit to speak with my mouth, I understood that my mind had nothing to do with what I was saying (1 Corinthians 14:14). As the days and weeks went by, the words began to flow more easily, and I could even sing in the unknown language. It was as if my spiritual life shifted into a higher gear. After all, Paul did both; he prayed and sang in the Holy Spirit (1 Corinthians 14:15). I became so much more in tune with God after I started releasing my tongue for His glory.

I am an analytical type and find it helpful to understand the principles behind how things work. The following, which was revealed to me soon after I began praying in this spiritual language, is what I understand to be going on when we pray in tongues.

1. Foundations have to be built for there to be steady, secure structures. Jesus told His disciples to go back to Jerusalem and wait for the power of the Holy Spirit before going out to witness. The first manifestation of the Holy Spirit that the disciples experienced was tongues of fire that settled on each one of them. "And they were filled throughout their souls and began to speak in other languages (tongues) as the spirit directed" (Acts 2).

   These tongues of fire and this first instance of tongues were foundational. And if this experience was that important to Jesus, shouldn't it be important for us to receive and pass on this spiritual mystery to others? After all, three thousand people became Christians that day (Acts 2).

2. God the Father's plan is for the Holy Spirit to move through all of us. Of course, He can do anything, but His plan is for the Holy Spirit to move through His children (Acts 2). Living water flows through us, and if water is released, it has to go somewhere (John 7:38).

3. If living water flows through us, it has to refresh and cleanse us.

The river of living water is not like the Mississippi River; it is more like a round pipe. When the living water flows through that pipe, it will clean out the riverbed. First, it will start washing away the sand that has accumulated because of the many rocks in the riverbed. After the sand is washed away, rocks will be exposed to the living water, and we will have to deal with these rocks (strongholds) in our lives. Otherwise, we will stop praying in the Spirit, and the sand will accumulate to protect the rock. The person who prays in tongues will change and be cleaned up the most.

4. The living water can flow to all nations.

Jesus started flowing His living waters on the day of Pentecost. Around my fifth year in prison, a group of Spanish Christians asked if I would meet them in the chapel at two o'clock one day. They wanted to pray that God would give someone the gift of interpretation of tongues. I thought, *God, not me.* I should have known better than to say that. As the men started praying in tongues, I started seeing these messages and pictures in my mind, but I waited for someone else to speak up. After a long silence, I knew I was on the spot and had to speak out about what I had seen and heard (1 Corinthians 12:10). I told them that God was saying our prayers were like rivers covering the nations. Our thoughts or the prison bars did not limit God's heavenly realm.

5. God will also from time to time tell us for whom we are praying. One day while working at my desk in the prison factory, praying quietly in tongues, I repeatedly heard the name Sheldon Williams in my mind. He was the father of one of my brother's friends. I didn't think much about it after that. That weekend, my parents came to visit and asked out of the blue if I'd heard about Sheldon Williams. My reply was, "No. How could I possibly know about anything while in prison?" They explained that just the other day he had caught his hand in a lawn mower. It happened at the exact time I was praying in tongues and heard his name. I later read a book by Kenneth Hagin, who taught that we could know who we were praying for in tongues if we were quiet and listened. That is true, but I don't stop to listen very often. I don't need to understand everything that is going on.

6. While in prison, I started praying for a list of approximately twenty people regularly and have continued to do this over the last twenty or so years. The names change as my life changes. I probably average praying five times per week. I write each name on an individual sheet of paper, and each time I pray, I note the date and then pray in tongues for a brief time. Then I write the thought that comes into my head. Living water leaves me and goes to each person's spirit realm. There are good and bad spirits fighting over each of them, and the living water feeds and encourages the spirits of God.

Then God tells me what He wants me to hear; sometimes He even tells me to go tell the person something, which, often with hesitation, I have obediently learned to do. If we can get in contact with others by a cell phone, why can't we speak and listen through God's heavenly channels?

7. When we pray in tongues, we really pray in tongues of fire (Acts 2:3).

On my fiftieth birthday, I was being transported through prison channels from Big Spring, Texas, to Tallahassee, Florida. It is not a direct flight, and my travel ended up taking weeks. I don't know how to explain what happened to me. It may be hard to understand what I am about to say without having experienced spiritual pressure from the enemy for such a long period of time.

I had to do a tremendous amount of fasting, eating only enough to have strength and remain spiritually sensitive. I had to pray in tongues six and seven hours per day just to stay alive. After several weeks, I finally arrived in Tallahassee, where the pressure was far more intense than I had previously experienced. I found a man named Ronnie to pray with me. We went to the chapel, knelt, and prayed quietly in tongues in the hall for an hour each day. One day while praying, I saw into the spiritual realm. Our prayers were like little bonfires. As the fires were burning, angels began to thaw from some frozen state and started moving. If you saw the first movie *The Chronicles of Narnia*, you have seen exactly what happened. As we prayed, the Lion of Judea roared, and the angels started moving again. How exciting it was. A few days later, the spirit over the entire prison changed.

8. We don't have to wait until the Spirit comes and forces us to pray in tongues. He doesn't force. Praying in tongues is like any prayer; we choose to pray or not. Usually we need to pray the most when we feel the worst. Other times, the Spirit moves on us, and we just find ourselves praying in tongues.

9. Spiritual prayers can be likened to shooting smart bombs into Satan's forces. They always hit the target and do massive amounts of damage.

You can believe Satan is going to do everything possible to try to stop the bombing. The modern-day Pharisees and Sadducees (preachers and teachers who do not use spiritual gifts or encourage others to use spiritual gifts) are aiding Satan in his efforts. "For [although] they hold a form of piety (true religion), they deny and reject and are strangers to the power of it [their conduct belies the genuineness of their profession]. Avoid [all] such people [turn away from them]" (2 Timothy 3:5).

10. When someone speaks in tongues, is it just a foreign language to us? I don't know. Paul said, "There are, I suppose, all these many [to us unknown] tongues in the world [somewhere], and none is destitute of [its own power of] expression and meaning" (1 Corinthians 14:10). I don't understand what I am saying when I pray in tongues, and I don't have to understand. One of our biggest obstacles to becoming Christlike is that we think we have to understand everything about something before we do it. If your boss asks you to buy ten milkshakes,

she doesn't have to tell you whom she is going to give them to. You just go buy the shakes because she told you to. Somehow, we think we can study and understand the things of God. Study is *part* of understanding the mysteries of God. God has hidden the truth from those who study and don't have the simple faith to trust and obey Him. If you don't believe that, go and read the account of the seventy. Their story can be found in Luke 10. In verse 21, Jesus said, *"I thank you, Father, Lord of heaven and earth, that You have concealed these things [relating to salvation] from the wise and understanding and learned, and revealed them to babes (the childish, unskilled, and untaught).* Yes, Father, for such was Your gracious will and choice and good pleasure" (emphasis added). If you wait to know and understand everything before you pray in an unknown tongue, you never will. Trust and obey, for there is no other way to be happy in Jesus.

11. Can satanic spirits speak in tongues through people not known to you? Certainly, they can and will. They will try to copy everything good that God created and make it perverse. Look what Satan has done with sex. If you are afraid to turn your tongue over to God's Spirit, let me assure you, there is nothing to worry about if you are born again. Go for it; you will be blessed and become a blessing. If you have not received Jesus as your Lord and Savior, be really careful. I have heard people who were of the wrong spirit speaking in unknown languages in church settings. Don't ever be fooled into believing Satan's angels can't get into church buildings and into people who attend the services, especially leaders. The choir is also a special place for them.

I now understand why Paul said, "I pray in tongues more than any of you" (1 Corinthians 14:18). He was wise enough to know that he didn't know the perfect will of God when he prayed.

God wants His kingdom expanded. Why would He want to limit the Holy Spirit from moving through all of His children? If you seek a prayer language with all your heart, you will receive it.

Why would someone not want to release the Holy Spirit upon those he loves? Why would someone not want to be built up and refreshed by the Holy Spirit? Why would someone not want to release the Holy Spirit into the lives of people all over the world? Can you imagine how frustrated God must be when we try to convince Him how to change our partners, other people, and circumstances and won't just release Him to do what He knows is best?

Please share this with your spiritual leader.

We Are Affected by Others— Even While in the Womb

Cissy and I were in a weeklong class held by Christian Healing Ministries in Jacksonville. The leaders said we were going to go through a conception-to-birth prayer. I thought this was way out, even for me. Immediately, God brought a memory to me.

While I was in prison, I had a prayer partner named Paul. We practiced praying about things together and hearing from God. His wife had told him that when he got out, he could come live with the family, but she would need to be the head of the house. He asked me to pray and ask God what the real problem was. I prayed and all I heard was *abortion*.

During Paul's next visit with his wife, he asked her if she had ever had an abortion. She was offended and became angry as he persisted; she had never had an abortion. When she got back home, she told her mother about Paul's accusation. Her mother said, "I need to tell you something. You are one of a pair of twins; I aborted the other baby and didn't know you were there until it was too late." From this experience, I knew that things that happen in a mother's womb affect her child.

The prayer at the retreat I was on with Cissy had us go on a journey with God through the nine months we were in the womb and experience what was going on. It was real, and everyone who prayed the prayer experienced the journey again.

Mother and Daddy were not Christians, and mother was not interested much in cuddling babies. God had provided for me with the maid who worked for the family at the time; she loved God and held and cuddled me. One woman in the retreat group had said all of her life she had wished she had never been born. She found out the reason. Her parents didn't want the responsibility of a child and gave her up for adoption.

That was a strange prayer experience, but its impact had more of an effect on the one hundred or more Christian leaders who were there that week for training than anything else.

When I start to disciple someone, one of the first things I do is take her through this birthing prayer. A copy of the prayer is at the end of this book.

How Could I Get Over What I Passed on to My Children?

When I was forty-two, I had really messed up my life and my children's lives as well. I was going through my fourth divorce and was out on bond, awaiting a prison sentence that would send me away for God only knows how long. Mother suggested that going to see a psychiatrist might be a good idea. I made an appointment, because there sure had to be a lot wrong with me.

During my first visit, the psychiatrist told me that most people had the same thoughts I had. I just carried out my thoughts without first thinking through the consequences. He recommended more appointments and said that the process could get expensive.

We agreed on weekday sessions at eight in the morning. This worked out well because one of my requirements for being out on bond was reporting to my parole officer, who was located in Valdosta, Georgia, every day during the week and by phone on the weekends. Valdosta is twenty-five miles from my home, which was in Madison, Florida. Madison was also where the psychiatrist's office was located.

During the first visit, I asked if he wanted me to sit in the chair or lie on the couch.

After all, in the movies, people in psychiatrists' offices were always on the couch. He said, "If you sit up, you will look to me for answers. On the couch, you will have to look inside yourself."

The couch seemed like the right place for me. On the way to the office and on the way home, I prayed in tongues, knowing that only with God's help could I go through this.

Things progressed rapidly as the tears flowed and the healing was taking place.

The psychiatrist said, "We are moving so fast that maybe we need to bring in a psychologist to make sure we are on the right track." The psychologist gave me some tests, pictures, and that kind of stuff, but never asked me any serious questions.

A few weeks later, the psychiatrist said that the psychologist's report was back and asked if I wanted to see the findings. I said of course I did. The report indicated that I had high tendencies for alcoholism, homicide, and homosexuality, among other very bad things. Homicide; that was me. I was headed to prison for paying someone to kill a man who had stolen a lot of money from our insider-trading venture. Everything named in that report was in my brothers, my sister, or me. The report described Daddy and Mother's personalities so accurately that it was like hitting a nail squarely on the head with a hammer. What a blow.

My concern was not about my parents, who had passed this junk on to us. I only wanted to forgive them, for they did not understand what they were doing to their children and grandchildren. My concern was that I was passing this junk on to my children. The iniquities in parents are passed on to the third and fourth generations (Exodus 20:5). My first thought was to kill myself and quit destroying my children's lives. On the way home, riding through the city of Valdosta, I said, "God, at least I'll be in prison and can't hurt them anymore."

God said, "Your children's stepfathers won't be any better, and your children are not their responsibility." At the railroad track, leaving town, my shirt was wet with tears. My tears were not tears of sadness, but tears of peace and hope and trust like I was raining while the sun was shining.

God spoke to me very gently and said, "Billy, you have the greatest opportunity in the world if you will just let me change you."

I had to choose whether to continue to be a conduit for this junk or a dam.

It has been a slow process of change, and now, after twenty-six years, He is still changing me. The Scripture that says, "get the plank out of your own eye, and you will see how to get the speck out of others'" sure rings true with parents and children (Luke 6:42). I was too busy trying to get my children to conform to my beliefs through my planks and didn't see the specks I was placing in their eyes that would grow to be planks. No matter how much harm we have done to our children, God gives us the greatest opportunities to right our wrongs if we just let Him change us.

I Just Couldn't Forgive Myself

I knew God had forgiven me for all the harm and pain I had caused my ex-wives and girlfriends. I was having a hard time forgiving myself. One night, two to three years into my prison stay, I had a dream. In the dream, all my ex-wives and girlfriends were standing around my bed.

In back of them there were filing drawers too numerous to count. In these drawers were the records of all I had done. Suddenly, the house caught on fire. We escaped, but all the records were burned up. God had burned them up.

The women will hold on to the records, however, until the scars in their hearts are healed.

The next day, God spoke to me through a story I read. There was a young boy named Johnny. He lied all the time, and each time his daddy caught him in a lie, he would put a nail in the barn door.

After a while, there were so many nails that the neighbors asked the daddy why he had put all those nails in the barn door. He explained that every time he caught Johnny in a lie, he put another nail in the barn door, and it started embarrassing Johnny. Johnny asked his daddy what he needed to do to get him to pull the nails out of the door. His daddy explained that if he would just go thirty days without lying, he would pull the nails out. The thirty days passed, and on that Saturday morning, Johnny was very happy and asked his daddy to pull the nails out of the door. As his daddy started pulling out the nails, Johnny started crying.

His daddy asked what the problem was. Johnny explained that though the nails were gone, the holes were still there.

God spoke to me through His small voice. He said, "Billy, my son, you have driven a lot of nails in those women's lives. You did your part when you repented and changed; the rest is up to them. The good news is I have pulled the nails out and the holes are open in them to receive my healing. There is nothing more you can do. Guilt after you repent and are forgiven only releases pain in the holes. If you hold on to the guilt, you don't think what Jesus did on the cross was enough to cover your sins and guilt." Guilt is a poison that will destroy relationships with spouses and especially with children. Everything done out of guilt is sin.

My God, Is This Spirit in Me?

I was in the chapel one day, and all these homosexual thoughts kept flooding my mind. I thought my brother was homosexual at one time, and it scared me. I went back to the dorm and started praying and asking God what was going on. He said, "The spirit was not in you, but in the group you were in." What a relief.

We can be attacked from spirits outside of us. If we are not careful, we will entertain those spirits and invite them into our lives. You hang around angry people and you may start getting angry. You hang around self-righteous people and if you're not careful, you might become self-righteous. God said to take every thought captive. That sure is a good policy. If you listen long enough to the spirits outside of you, they will come into you. If you don't examine where thoughts come from, they will destroy you and your relationships. If you listen long enough to anything, you will start to believe it, and it will become a part of you.

Who Are the Self-righteous?

Before I became a Christian, I used to think the self-righteous people were those in church who talked one way and did another. The non-church crowd I was part of used that example all the time. I started to think about all those times at the bar when we would say that if it were not for our wives, we would be home. Then we would talk about how they didn't appreciate us, especially us workaholics.

Then I started thinking about how so much of our conversation was about running others down. We were all saying that we were right and they were wrong by our standards.

We are all a group of self-righteous individuals by God's standard, His laws. I just thank God for His grace. He has put up with so much mess from me.

There is a relevant story in the Bible about this self-righteousness:

> Two men went up into the temple [enclosure] to pray, the one a Pharisee and the other a tax collector. The Pharisee took his stand ostentatiously and began to pray thus before and with himself: God, I thank You that I am not like the rest of men—extortioners (robbers), swindlers [unrighteous in heart and life], adulterers—or even like this tax collector here. I fast twice a week; I give tithes of all that I gain.
>
> But the tax collector, [merely] standing at a distance, would not even lift up his eyes to heaven, but kept striking his breast, saying, O God, be favorable (be gracious, be merciful) to me, the especially wicked sinner that I am!
>
> I tell you, this man went down to his home justified (forgiven and made upright and in right standing with God), rather than the other man; for everyone who exalts himself will be humbled, but he who humbles himself will be exalted. (Luke 18:10–14)

Let me tell you a story about my self-righteousness. After accepting Christ, I was like a drunk who had just sobered up.

I wanted everyone to accept Christ, and if they didn't, they were as crazy as I had been. I could not understand why they didn't listen. Of course, it only took more than forty years for me to listen. Here I was going to prison, abandoning my children and leaving the responsibility of raising them to someone else.

I was giving the impression that I had it all and telling people, "Y'all are nothing without Christ."

After three years of my sermons to my sons' mothers I woke up one day and took a look at myself.

After a little talk with Jesus, I told my son Will's mother that I needed to talk to her. Usually she was very short and angry, as she should have been. I thanked her for her and her husband looking after Will and asked her to forgive me for abandoning my responsibilities. After that I had a hard time getting her off the phone to talk to Will.

Which time did I really share Jesus with her: when I was self-righteously preaching or when I was asking for forgiveness? Self-righteousness is a knife that will stick into the hearts of everyone you come in contact with, and it will run people away from Jesus.

My Brother Dan Made It to Heaven!

Dan was the youngest of my siblings. He was special, but my siblings and I didn't understand him. He was not interested in football or baseball; he liked tumbling and acrobatics. Daddy kept encouraging him to do the things that most boys were doing, so Dan did play the sports that were popular, but his heart was not in them. He later went to Florida State University, where he was part of the circus and loved it. After graduation, he went to work for a state agency and rose to the top very fast—too fast. The newly elected head of the agency replaced him because his position was not protected. Along with the job loss, he went through a divorce. His life started a downward spiral that lasted a long time.

Dan got involved in some very bad stuff, including homosexuality. This happens all too often when a young boy has been molested. Through the prison ministry I have been involved in on a biweekly basis for years, I have to deal with this regularly. There are very few men who are now in prison for sexual crimes who were not molested. Mother had an uncle who had never been married and who spent his vacations with us and slept in the same room with Dan. Mother and Daddy did not have a clue as to what could happen or the consequences.

With the help of a Christian group, Dan seemed to pull himself back together. He went to work for a bank as a mortgage broker and was very successful. The bank tested him and found out that he had the IQ of a genius. A very nice lady who was a preacher's daughter moved in with him, but their relationship didn't last much more than a year. Dan had taken out disability insurance and had done so well that when he found out that he was terminally ill with AIDS, he drew more than five thousand dollars per month in disability payments, which was a lot of money twenty years ago. He died several years later.

I was in prison during the last years of my brother's life. I would like to share with you what I heard from God and others during this time.

There was a man in prison who had an artificial leg. In the visiting room, he would hide cocaine in the leg to sell in prison. An inmate told the prison officials what was going on. We worked in a woodworking shop together, and at the time, an officer saw him making himself a knife out of plastic to protect himself that morning. After lunch, the rest of us in the shop were sent back to the dorm while the officer arrested him and put him in the jail inside the prison.

Back in the dorm, I was lying on my bunk, taking a nap, during which I had a dream or a vision. I was outside Jesus' tomb and saw an angel on top of the stone saying, "He is not here; He has risen." I didn't know what the meaning was at the time, but somehow I knew I was going home in two years, before the date the parole board had set, and it was not going to be a pleasant experience. I shared this with Mother and Daddy. They were excited about my coming home, but not as excited about the unpleasant experience I anticipated.

I wrote Dan a letter and asked him to make contact with the lady he had lived with, to tell her what was going on and to ask her to forgive him. He didn't have the strength to write another letter back to me, but he wrote notes on the letter I had written him. He said there was no need to contact her.

Mother called to tell me that Dan was going to die, which I already knew.

That evening on the recreation yard, I cried out to God to heal Dan so Mother and Daddy would know He was real. God spoke through the inner voice that I knew to be Him and said, "Dan is going to die, but I will give you the sign of Jonah." My reaction was, "What in the world is the sign of Jonah?" Of course, it is repentance.

The lady Dan had lived with told me that sometimes Dan spoke out of seven different personalities. Mother told me that in the latter stages of his disease, Dan cursed her with words she had never heard. It didn't seem to me that there was any chance of him going to heaven with all the demons in him.

Mother called the prison in advance of Dan's death to make arrangements for me to come home to the funeral. They informed her I would be accompanied by a guard and would have handcuffs and leg irons on.

I didn't want to embarrass my family by coming home in that condition. In the federal prison system, an inmate can choose whether to see the family member before death or go to the funeral. Dan was in hospice in Tallahassee where I was, so the prison staff arranged for me to go see him there.

On the morning of the scheduled visit, Mother called to tell me Dan had left the hospice unit the night before, weighing ninety pounds and carrying his television on his back. Nobody knew where he was for days. One day he showed up at home. He died around a month later at his home.

After Dan's death, the prison staff arranged for me to go home without handcuffs or leg irons. What was even better was that a guard at the prison had lived next door to Mother and Daddy when he was growing up, and he escorted me to the funeral. Before the church service that morning, the lady Dan had lived with came to the house. She explained she had seen the notice in the paper. I told her I needed to talk with her. After all, she had been exposed to AIDS and needed to know. She told me she had been tested and was clear. Dan had found her unlisted phone number, called her two weeks before, and asked her to forgive him for everything. There it was: the sign of Jonah. Dan had repented, just as God had promised!

The funeral arrangements were made so I could spend as much time with my children as possible. The memorial service was held at the church in the morning, followed by lunch for friends and family at the house, and then we held a family burial after lunch.

At the burial, Dan's urn was directly in front of me. As I was meditating on what God had promised me about him, I heard that still small voice say, "What did I show you two years ago?" It had been two years ago to the day and hour that I had had the vision of Jesus' tomb and the angel saying, "He has risen." Dan's funeral was not a pleasant experience. However, God said, "Don't worry. He is with me, and he has risen just as I promised two years ago." Dan is in heaven, wanting me to tell others about the Jesus he is with. Our family was so spiritually blind, we didn't have a clue what was going on or how to find spiritual help for Dan.

Jesus suffered and died to heal and to set people like Dan free. The framework for those prayers can be found at, stepstohealingamerica.com.

Jesus Is at the Door Knocking; Don't Be Afraid to Let Him In

Jesus says, "Behold, I stand at the door and knock; if anyone hears and listens to and heeds My voice and opens the door, I will come in to him and will eat with him, and he [will eat] with Me" (Revelation 3:20).

At first I had a problem letting Jesus in to chat with me. I was like so many who are afraid. I thought Jesus just wanted to tell me everything I was doing wrong and tell me to straighten out or He was going to punish me until I started changing. After all, why shouldn't we think that way? Most parents tell their children twenty things the kids do wrong for every one thing the kids do right. Most of us have never been told how good we are or have been thanked by our parents for doing something good. So it is easy to form a picture of Jesus based on the way people, especially our parents, have treated us.

However, Jesus actually died for us. The Bible tells us, "For God *did not send the Son into the world in order to judge (to reject, to condemn, to pass sentence* on) the world, but that the world might find salvation and *be made safe and sound through Him*" (John 3:17, emphasis added).

Jesus wants to love, heal, and forgive us so we can be the people we were created to be in the first place.

So many of us have been taught to believe and commit our lives to a Jesus we really don't know. He wants us to get to know Him personally—not just read about Him or listen to someone tell us about Him. I asked an inmate the other day if, when he was released, he would go to a judge's office and commit his life to a woman he had only read about. If he had read a book about her and heard someone speak who had read a book about her, would he marry her? He said no, of course, because he had not met her and didn't *really* know her. Jesus wants you to get to know Him and understand His power before you make up your mind about whether you want to commit your life to Him and be a part of His family. You will never know Him until you open the door to Him.

Have You Ever Felt
Abandoned and Alone?

Being abandoned is one of the biggest causes of pain and emotional bruising. How does a child feel when her parents get divorced? How does the mate who was abandoned through divorce feel? How does a child feel when a parent favors one child over the other? How does a child feel who is given up for adoption or put in a foster home? How does a child feel when a parent goes to prison, as I did? I left behind a tender-hearted little boy whose feelings became locked up inside and who stopped crying.

During visits, one son would try to show me how to break out and would hold on to me for dear life when leaving the visiting room. He would say, "Daddy, I need you at home with us; you have abandoned us." There were times when there were no visits because the pain was too great for my children. It was too much guilt to bear, so I just built another internal prison cell to protect my pain and shame.

It wasn't until several years ago that I had the courage to open that door for Jesus to bring me truth and healing. Up until that time, when those times in the visiting room were mentioned, I would start crying because of the pain and guilt. I sat in my recliner and said, "God, it is time for us to deal with this," as I quietly sat there with tears coming out of my eyes. I saw a picture in my mind of myself back in that visiting room with my son Caleb hanging on to my leg. He was crying, I was crying, and Jesus was standing beside me and also crying. I heard that small voice. He said, "Billy, this was never my plan for you or your children. However, I promise you if you will stick with me and be as crazy for me as you have been for other things, I will dry up the tears in your children's hearts."

Many people think I am crazy, but if they think their words or thoughts are more important to me than healing the tears in my children's hearts, then they are the ones who are crazy.

There is a woman who helps me with clerical work. Her granddaughter is nine years old now and lives with her, her husband, and her parents (the granddaughter's great-grandparents). The little girl's mother left her when she was one year old and has not been back. Her father went from girlfriend to girlfriend. The grandparents, wanting to keep her daddy a part of her life because they thought they were doing the right thing, would let the little girl go to her dad's from time to time. Sometimes on the weekend the dad would have to work, and one of his girlfriends would lock the child in a dark closet or put her in a bathtub of cold water and make her stay there until just before her daddy came home. The little girl never told anyone these details; she just said that she did not want to go to her daddy's anymore. The daddy had issues from his childhood because his mother went to prison when he was very young, and he was a violent sort who would go off at the drop of a hat. He would always take the side of his girlfriends over his daughter or mother.

Only when the little girl knew this woman was out of her daddy's life forever did she tell what had been happening. Her father now has a new girlfriend who has four children of her own, and they now have another child together, so the little girl has a half-brother, two stepsisters, and two stepbrothers. She has told her grandmother that she always gets in trouble with her daddy because the woman he lives with continually says she is doing things that she is not. She asks us not to tell anyone, out of fear of what her daddy may do, so she does not go to his house that often these days. She says she's sorry at the drop of a hat, no matter what she has done. She feels no one loves her, although she has been the center of her grandparents' and great-grandparents' world since birth. She feels totally abandoned by both her mother and father and feels that her father favors his new son and the other children who now live with him. She feels he does not love her at all.

This child is so emotionally bruised, she will never get over her pain without the help of spiritual healing from Jesus. She is very vulnerable to pain and wants very much to be loved by her real mom and dad. It is such a sad situation, and no matter how much her grandparents love this child or do for this child, she still feels no one really loves her the way she wants or needs to be loved. She desires to be loved unconditionally, especially by her mother. However, her mom has not been around in eight years. She wants to be loved unconditionally by her father, but all he does is chastise her instead of trying to love her for the beautiful, smart, and sensitive little girl that she is.

The little girl asked her grandmother one day, "Why does God let people live that do not have any friends?"

Her grandmother responded, "Because God loves you, and He can be your best friend. He does not tell your secrets, He listens, He loves you unconditionally, no matter what, and He is always with you." Her grandmother went on to explain that people do not always need friends. "Friends sometimes let you down and hurt you just as bad as you feel your mom and daddy have."

The little girl seemed to accept this and has never mentioned it again. Every now and then, she will talk about how much she hates her life, and her grandmother just tells her how lucky Grandma is that she is in her life. She tells the little girl that she is thankful to have a little girl, since she had only had boys in the past. The grandmother says that God sent the little girl as a special angel for her.

Please be careful with your children. They are precious and vulnerable, and they learn by example. There are too many ways children are bruised that we are totally unaware of, such as bruises by their parents, siblings, step-siblings, kids at school, and the list goes on. This grandmother did not realize what her life had done to her sons until they were grown, and now, in turn, her granddaughter is suffering with bruises, deep emotional scars, and pain.

The sad part is that the grandmother was offered help and never accepted it. We can't help others find freedom and peace until we have found it for ourselves. We will attempt to help others on the wrong side of the cross while we are still suffering. True help can only be given on the resurrected side, where there is joy.

Over the last twenty-five years, I have never met someone who had been adopted who did not ask, "What is wrong with me that my parents didn't want me?" Then there are those whose parents got divorced and one parent abandoned them; the question in that case is always, "What is wrong with me that my own parent does not want me?" These bruises are carried on for the rest of the children's lives, and the parents' mistakes are passed on for generations (Exodus 20:5).

You will feel abandoned and alone when sleeping next to your mate unless Jesus heals the bruises that separate you. Jesus suffered and died to heal our bruises. He didn't suffer and die to tell us how to live with our bruises.

Suggested prayer for those who were abandoned and alone can be found at stepstohealingamerica.com.

How Many People Are in Your Bed?

The number of people in your bed is the number of people you've had sexual relationships with. Every one of them is joined to you. It's not surprising, then, that sexual issues are probably the deepest issues that need addressing in nearly everyone's life.

A woman's womb is a picture of the Holy of Holies, the most sacred inner chamber of a place of worship. When Jesus' blood was shed on the cross, the curtain to the Holy of Holies was torn open; now everyone who has made a life commitment to Him can enter that place of holiness. Jesus' death opened the way for new life in us. Blood has to be shed and the curtain covering the most intimate place in a woman must be ripped open before life can begin. A woman's intimate place is sacred and should only be entered by someone who has made a lifelong commitment to her. It takes a true life commitment for one to be born again and for new life to come into us. Men become one with every woman's intimate parts they enter. When we contaminate that temple, we contaminate all life and relationships that are born there. Everyone who enters that scared place deposits his gods (spirits) in that temple. Those gods (spirits) are deposited into everyone who enters that temple. No wonder our children are so messed up and our relationships are failing. Jesus cleansed the temple in Jerusalem, and He can cleanse our temples too.

If the temples are not cleansed, you will most likely experience having sex with your life partner while thinking about someone you have had intercourse with in the past. You may not think that is so bad, but remember that your partner could be thinking about someone else also. No one in her right mind wants to be sharing intimately with her partner while he is thinking about someone else. This becomes really tragic when someone has been sexually molested and finds himself having thoughts of his molester. This is a big bruise that will certainly destroy a marriage and family if not healed.

When we look at adultery through God's eyes, the picture is a lot different from the way we typically see it. As Matthew 5:28 says, "Everyone who so much as looks at a woman with evil desire for her has already committed adultery with her in his heart." We are all guilty of adultery if we have not repented of past sexual relationships. If you have not gone to God and received a heavenly douche or heavenly circumcision, you are probably providing fuel for your partner's fire, and then you are both guilty of adultery in God's eyes.

Remember, until we get our hearts right, God's blood can't flow through us and into any situation. 1 Corinthians 1:18 reminds us to "shun immorality and all sexual looseness [flee from impurity in thought, word, or deed].

Any other sin which a man commits is one outside the body, but he who commits sexual immorality sins against his own body."

Further, according to *The Message* a paraphrase of the Bible:

> There is more to sex than mere skin on skin. Sex is as much spiritual mystery as physical fact. As written in Scripture, "the two become one." Since we want to become spiritually one with the Master, we must not pursue the kind of sex that avoids commitment and intimacy, leaving us lonelier than ever—the kind of sex that can never embrace each other. There is a sense in which sexual sins are different from all others. In sexual sin, we violate the sacredness of our own bodies, these bodies that were made for God-given and God-modeled love, for "becoming one" with another. Or didn't you realize that your body is a sacred place, the place of the Holy Spirit? Don't you see that you can't live however you please, squandering what God paid such a high price for? The physical part of you is not some piece of property belonging to the spiritual part of you. God owns the whole works. So let people see God in and through your body. (1 Corinthians 6:16-20)

We can't leave this subject without addressing sexual molestation, which is one of the most damaging things that can happen in a person's life. Molestation happens to a lot more people than you would ever imagine. More than twenty five per cent of all women and twenty per cent of all men have been sexually molested. Half of the men were molested by older women. When you enter a relationship with someone who has been molested, the relationship will be torn apart unless your partner's molestation is dealt with.

I have never met someone who was molested who didn't blame herself. I don't know whether any of these people were partly responsible or not. Jesus was there when it happened, and He is the only one who knows the truth. I just say if you will go back to the incident and invite Jesus in, He will tell you the truth. If it was your fault, you can repent. If it was not your fault, then you will finally know the truth from the only one who knows. As long as those who have been molested believe a lie, the condemning spirit has a right to stay in them. When they know the truth and accept it, the spirit has to leave because it loses its legal right to stay. Let freedom ring. Those who have been molested will no longer have to feel dirty, ugly, and unworthy of having a decent mate.

The sexual problems your partner has are now your problems, also, because you have chosen to be become one. These are now family issues that must not be swept under the rug.

You can be sympathetic and caring enough to understand the problem, but a pity party will not eliminate the gorilla that lives in your family.

You should have compassion and be courageous, going to God for help dealing with it. If you don't start listening to God, your anger and resentment toward your partner as she rejects you will produce a poison that will destroy the whole family. It is a spiritual poison that needs a doctor, and the only doctor who has the healing medicine is Jesus. A counselor, psychologist, or psychiatrist can help you identify the pain; only Jesus can heal it.

A partner of a victim will feel rejected when the frigid person goes back to his pain. The victim may even disassociate himself, as he has surely learned to do, and although you are having intercourse with him, it is as if he is not really there. You will feel very rejected and believe the problem is you, because you have now become one with that gorilla, and he will tell you so.

Men who have been sexually molested by older women usually think it was a good thing, because the women taught them how to be men. Some then only find themselves wanting older street women, strippers, or hookers, even when they have good wives at home. Deep inside, these men know they need a good woman. They will try to change good women into street women or they will try to change unrepentant street women into good women, and they will only fail. Their wives will feel sexually unworthy; our churches are full of those women who wear nice clothes and carry a false smile to hide the emptiness and unworthiness they feel inside. Their husbands' issues had nothing to do with them; the cause was the sexual imprinting the man received before being married.

During my stay in federal prison, I was placed in a prison where there were seventeen hundred women and five hundred men. We were basically with the women from seven in the morning until nine at night, when they returned to their dorms and we returned to ours.

What percentage of those women, do you think, were sexually molested before the age of sixteen? Let's say 75 percent, which is a low number; I know, I spent a year in prison with them and listened to them as they told their stories. How many do you think went to a church seeking help before coming to prison? All the ones I talked to.

If the church group even talked about it with these women, the church group just told them that they needed to forgive the person and move on with their lives. When they were molested, however, the molester's demon entered them.

Did the church people help get the demon or demons out or advise them on how to live with the pain? What would your church group do? When we laid hands on these women in the name of Jesus, the demons came out, and they were free to be little girls again. Molestation had robbed them of their childhoods. Most statistics I have read indicate that 70 to 80 percent of those who have been molested are on drugs or alcohol to numb the pain and cover the shame.

You would be hard-pressed to find a person who has committed a sexual crime who was not molested or a survivor of incest.

As 1 John 1:9 tells us, "If we [freely] admit that we have sinned and confess our sins, He is faithful and just (true to His own nature and promises) and will forgive our sins [dismiss our lawlessness] and [continuously] cleanse us from all unrighteousness [everything not in conformity to His will in purpose, thought, and action]." We need to be cleansed of our mistakes. He can cleanse us if we do not continue to sweep the pain and false pleasures under the rug.

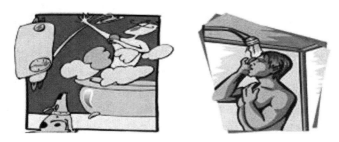

In lay terms, He will give women heavenly douches and men heavenly circumcisions. Then they will be spiritually cleaned to become one with the people they are committed to as God intended.

My first experience of being free from a past relationship came before I went to prison, while I was still out on bond. I was going to a strange church that had a ministry called "life counseling." They prayed about different things in people's lives. One person would lead while the others prayed in tongues. They searched around in my life and said I had been set free of a lot of stuff by going to the psychiatrist, but there seemed to be one thing left that God wanted to deal with: my relationship with my first girlfriend, the one I had had sexual relations with. She was the wife who had just divorced me. When they prayed for me, her spirit came out of me.

Water came out of my eyes, nose, and ears. I had never experienced anything like that before. I was a new Christian, but I knew something dramatic had happened. I wrote her a letter and said, "I don't understand what happened today when those people prayed for me. However, the spiritual connection I had with you has disappeared. I am now free to go on with my life and a new relationship."

The week before those people prayed for me, my mother had asked me to take her vacuum cleaner to be repaired. The repair place was right across the street from the apartment complex my ex-wife managed. I felt the spirit of rejection come over me and couldn't believe what was happening. After they prayed for me, I went back to pick up that vacuum cleaner and went to the apartment where my ex-wife was, to pick up some furniture, and it was as if I was with a stranger. Her spirit was no longer in me, and there was no attachment there.

Since that time, the power of the Holy Spirit has taken all of the others I have had sex with away from me when I repented and invited Him in to bring me truth and healing. I believe in this process because of the many people I have prayed with who were similarly set free. Until that happens, it is impossible to have a full relationship with God or our mates.

How can a relationship work in which the man has become one with ten women and the woman has become one with five men? One couple is trying to make a relationship work between seventeen people. It is hard enough for two to become one, much less accommodating seventeen people in the same marriage bed. How many people are in your marriage bed? If you are not married, how many people will be in bed with you when you get married? Do your church leaders offer sexual cleansing before marrying a couple? Sexual cleansing was never mentioned any of the five times I got married in a church, and yet most women need a heavenly douche, and most men need to be heavenly circumcised.

Suggested prayers for sexual cleansing are at the end of the book.

What Do We Do for All the Drug Addicts and Alcoholics?

Why do people change personalities when they drink or use drugs? The drugs or alcohol only cause people to relax, so whatever personality comes out was already in them. It is called a demon. Buzzards feed on dead meat, just as demons feed on the bruises in our lives. The drug or alcohol addicts have been deeply bruised. They don't have to deal with the pain while intoxicated, and the demon spirits get to just run wild. When their bruises are healed, there won't be a need for drugs or alcohol. When spiritual bruises are present and alcohol or drugs act as the solution, there will never be peace in the addict's relationships. Jesus died to heal our bruises and cast out our demons.

Do you believe in demons? Do your church leaders cast out demons, as Jesus commanded, or do they just try to get the person off drugs or alcohol? Treating the person instead of the demon is like giving someone an aspirin for terminal cancer.

What Is All This Fuss about Smoking?

A man came up to me and asked me to pray with him about his smoking. This was my first time meeting him. He said God was just beating him up about it. As I prayed, I realized it was not God but his religious friends. Then I told him God was not concerned about his smoking right now; he needed to forgive his mother. He cried out, "I have not spoken to her in ten years!" What do you think God was concerned about?

My roommate in prison and I had been together for three years when he was sent to another prison to have an operation at the prison's hospital. Another man came to me and asked if he could move in with me. I didn't answer him at that time because I knew he smoked about two packs per day, and I had quit after I got sick smoking a cigar at the age of sixteen. Then I thought I'd just pray about it. *What a mistake,* I thought as God spoke to me. He said, "There is going to be a separation one day, and it isn't going to be between smokers and non-smokers."

This man turned out to be one of the finest Christian men I have ever known. He still keeps in touch with me every year or so, and he is still serving Jesus twenty years later.

In a class several years ago, I met a man who condemned himself for not stopping his daddy from beating his mother. He was in prison, in fact, because he hurt men who beat women.

As he let Jesus deal with him, he stopped condemning himself and became free. He automatically quit smoking, and he had been smoking two packs per day.

Most of the time, we want to deal with symptoms in our lives and others' lives, but we fail to address the real problems underneath. Majoring on the minor and neglecting the major is easy to do when one is blind and can't see through Jesus' eyes. What guilt have your friends put on you that Jesus will take away when you do address your real issues?

Do You Understand the Effects
That Abortions Have on Families?

Back in prison twenty-two or so years ago, some of the first young men who blew up an abortion clinic arrived at the prison. I thought they were wrong and a bunch of misled fanatics. After I took the time to get to know them, I discovered that they were two very serious young Christians who were around a group of people who didn't have much maturity. They were very nice and polite, but they were also a lot like young gladiators.

For the first time, I understood how wrong the law that allows legal abortions is. One day, I decided to have a little talk with Jesus about abortions. At the time, I was working in food service, washing pots and pans. During a break, I said, "God, if you have all power, why don't you just change the law?"

His reply was, "There is only one reason for an abortion." Of course, I didn't know the reason. After a few days of meditating, the answer came: no one wanted to take responsibility for the baby. He said, "You got it."

He then continued: "When the people who call themselves by my name start taking responsibility for the ones who receive my seed, abortions will dwindle, and the law will change. Marching and protesting is man's way to remedy the abortion problem. My way is adoption. This is something most church leaders and the people who attend church don't seem to know about. They don't know me or trust my plan to spread the good news of salvation" (see Matthew 28:19–20).

I had no idea how serious the problem was until I started looking at some statistics. There were more babies murdered the week of 9/11 than there were adults who died in the plane bombings that day. However, we got all upset and went to war over the bombings to protect ourselves from the terrorists. We were responding through the eyes of men, not God.

Who does God see as the terrorists? We should have repented like the people of Nineveh (Jonah). Here we are, murdering more babies than any other democracy that has ever existed on this earth, and we have the nerve to call ourselves a Christian nation. Rather than repent, we send our young people to get mangled and die so other nations can build democracies that will condone killing babies like we do. Do you know that abortion is one of the main reasons the Muslims call us "the great Satan"? Are they wrong? After all, the squadron that bombed Baghdad the first time was named the Warlocks. It sure sounds like Satan attacking Satan. Maybe we need to get the plank out of our own eyes before trying to remove the speck in other nations' eyes. As the Bible says, "If My people, who are called by My name, shall humble themselves, pray, *seek, crave, and require of necessity My face* and turn from their wicked ways, then will I hear from heaven, forgive their sin, and heal their land" (2 Chronicles 7:14, emphasis added).

Our dollar bills say "in God we trust," but it seems we have put our trust in the dollar rather than in God.

Abortions are ripping the fabric of our society apart. One of the leading pro-life attorneys at a conference in Jacksonville said that 40 percent of the women in North America—that includes Mexico and Canada—have had an abortion. How can a person ever be the parent God planned him to be with the blood of a baby on his hands? Can someone who had an abortion ever have true peace in her life to pass on to her children? How can a person claim to have a personal relationship with Jesus and not aggressively work at God's remedy to save our children? Spiritual adoption.

We have a forgiver, a redeemer, and His name is Jesus. His desire is to forgive and heal, if that is really what you want. You will have to face the fact that you are a murderer and deserve to die. It might be a good idea to go spend a few nights in a jail cell or watch an execution to begin to understand the penalty for murder. You will have to change your way of thinking about everything and start looking through God's eyes, jump into His arms like a child wanting to be rescued. Then He will heal and forgive. He is the only one who can.

I read an interesting section from a book this morning, *Heaven Is So Real,* by Choo Thomas. On page 38, Thomas explains that all aborted babies, babies whose parents didn't want them, are in heaven with Jesus. She talks to Jesus and reports that He is very angry about abortion. He tells her that if the mother of an aborted baby gets to heaven and becomes His child, the mother can have her baby back. He will give the others to someone else. Thomas quotes a frightening statistic in her book: nearly one in four pregnancies in the United States ends in murder.

Jesus is a loving and healing God. Please take this message to your spiritual leader and encourage your group of believers to become a healing community that adopts and disciples. If your group needs help with learning how to be a healing community, I recommend getting in touch with the Christian Healing Center in Jacksonville, Florida.

Do You Think Christian Prayers Are the Only Ones That Have Power?

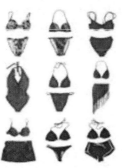

When people covet child pornography, why do you think they want those pictures? Do you think it stops with the picture? The picture gives them a spiritual line to the person in the picture, and what they do or fantasize about doing affects the person in the picture.

People who are sexually perverted in prison fight for pictures of young children in the newspaper or magazines in the same way they fight for all types of pornography. Parents who dress up their little girls for beauty contests and dance recitals have no idea what they are exposing them to.

Why do you think some Muslim sects require women to be covered? Is it because they have a better understanding of spiritual matters than we so-called enlightened people in the West? They know what happens when men start praying over their wives and daughters.

Women and girls who dress in enticing and exposing ways usually do not consider that they are not only attracting the individuals they want to attract.

A man who worked with me said his girlfriend and her friend were taking a shower at the beach and a man, whom they called a pervert, was taking pictures of them. They got all upset and wanted to call the police. I said, "What did they expect when they walked around nearly naked?" They gave him an engraved invitation to take those pictures.

Men and women will prey on scantily clad women, and their satanic sides have power. People are taking pictures in their minds all the time whether we like it or not.

The power of non-Christian prayer is not only evident when it comes to lust, however. When parents speak bad things over their children, they encourage bad spirits to take action. When people wish for or try to create bad things to happen to each other, bad things can happen.

More than twenty-seven years ago, before I became a Christian, my ex-wife was dating an alcoholic, and they were considering getting married. I had done everything I knew how to do in order to discourage the relationship.

There was a woman working for me who advised me that she knew a root man—a witch doctor—who could break them up. We went to a shack that was down a dirt road into the woods. There were cars parked around the yard. We waited for our turn. I told the man my concern. He told me to write my ex-wife and her boyfriend's names on a raw egg, put a small hole in the bottom of the egg, and place it in a red ant bed. I left him a one hundred-dollar bill, as expected and promptly put four eggs in four different red ant beds. After all, if one is good, four would be better. They broke up the next day.

While in prison in Lexington, Kentucky, I saw a man from Iran who had all kinds of feathers and animal feet hung around his neck. This man had money, and when he was arrested, there was a million dollars in the trunk of his car. He would go out several times per day to pray and do yoga.

One day I said, "Lord, what is he doing?"

God said, "He is having an out-of-body experience, directing spirits."

I get skeptical sometimes and try to get confirmation on what I think I have heard. I asked a lady who worked with this man to ask him what he was doing during his prayer time. He confirmed he was going outside his body and directing spirits. I said, "God, I better try to understand this."

God said, "You'd better; he is directing the spirits at you."

I said, "Who is directing your spirits?"

He said, "No one."

I knew from the Bible that when they came to arrest Jesus, Peter cut the guard's ear off. Jesus said, "Don't you know if I asked my Father, He would send twelve legions of angels to put at my disposal?" I thought I needed to ask God to send me some angels and to instruct me on what I should tell them to do.

That man convinced the chaplain to have a universal service. He invited his spiritual guide to lead a service and paid to have her flown from California. He had told people during the service that they would have an out-of-body experience. Some were excited. The woman came that morning and sang "How Great Thou Art" in the church choir. A group of Christians had been praying against the service that afternoon, and after fifteen minutes, 80 percent of the people walked out of the service.

The Iranian man's eyes were as black as the ace of spades.

I could walk within two feet of him, and he couldn't look at me. There is power in us from the blood of Jesus, but never forget Satan's power in his followers. When Satan's followers pray against others and us, we need to pray back with Jesus.

Do you think prayer from the wrong side that goes undetected can ruin lives and families? How have prayers from the other side affected you and your family?

Who Was Really Behind the Attack on the World Trade Center?

Most people have an opinion about what led to the attack on 9/11 and what we should do to protect ourselves. I would like to share with you what I believe God showed and told me. It is up to you decide whether you believe I heard from God or not.

Seven months before 9/11, I went every day to pray at a spiritual high place in Valdosta, Georgia. I had to ride a bicycle because a car could not go there. On 9/11, I had a piece of paper with me with the word "greed" written on it. I felt like it was the day to pray about the spirit of greed over Valdosta. On the way there, the Lord kept saying "New York City, New York City."

I said, "What about New York City?"

As I began to pray, I had a vision, and whether I was in my body or out of my body, I don't know. What I do know is that I was in the air, looking down on the financial district in New York City, especially the World Trade Center towers. God said in His gentle voice inside me, "You are looking at the *world center of greed, my enemy*." I told my wife and several others about what happened that day.

After the attack, I said, "God, you gave me the vision for a reason."

God said, "The World Trade Center towers housed the world center of greed, my enemy, so I sent the bombers. They were like a bat in a batter's hand, moving at my directions and under my power. This is the first pain of childbirth. The first pains don't come as often, nor are they as severe. No one can build an army big enough or design enough gadgets to prevent the rest that is on the way."

Remember that God destroyed the city and Tower of Babel in Genesis 1–9. The Babylonians said, "Let us build us a city and a tower whose top reaches into the sky, and let us make a name for ourselves." Nothing is left of their tower or city anymore.

God continued to speak to me: "The only thing that can prevent the rest of my punishment, which is a warning for your own good, is for the people who call themselves by my name to repent and turn from their wicked ways. Unless they do this, the rest of my punishment is on the way." He said to me, "Go warn the people that call themselves by my name."

I said, "Lord, they will think I am crazy, which most people already do."

He said, "Just ask them one question: hasn't their nation rejected me as their God? They now worship the gods of materialism. How many couples have bowed before my son Jesus and asked me if they should abort their child, and I said yes? Y'all are murdering more innocent children than any nation that has had the nerve to call itself by my name. What do you expect me to do? Sit by and do nothing? After all, why are you so surprised? I just answered my children's prayers to deliver them from evil."

I really feel this was from God because He sent evil nations against Israel when they turned from Him. It is also in harmony with what He said in the Bible: "If the people who are called by my name, shall humble themselves, pray, seek, crave, and require on necessity My face and turn from their wicked ways, then will I hear from heaven, forgive their sin, and heal their land" (2 Chronicles 7:14). We are a nation that needs healing. Who is preventing our healing, the terrorists or the people who call themselves by God's name?

Church people need to stop pointing fingers at the government and start praying for them; they will be more effective in bringing in Christian leaders into government positions. The church house needs new leadership a lot more than government does.

We need to get the plank out of our own eyes before we try to remove the splinter in other nations' eyes. We put bounties on Bin Laden, wanted dead or alive, and we hanged Saddam Hussein for ordering the killing of thousands of people. Meanwhile, we have legalized the murder of millions each year. How can we expect to escape the judgment of God?

Taking our eyes off God and turning toward material things will ultimately destroy all people and nations.

How Lukewarm Have We Become?

This Christmas I decided to do a lot of listening and not so much talking, which is against my nature.

We went to spend Christmas Eve and Christmas with one of our children and some of our grandchildren.

We had a pleasant two days together. The sad part was, except for a word or blessing over the food, the name of Jesus was never mentioned.

How could we be celebrating the birth of the one who is supposed to be the most important person in our lives and never mention His name?

How would you like to go to your birthday party, where you were ignored and people brought presents for everyone but you? It seems like a common affair in most so-called Christian homes that Jesus is not the center of attention on Christmas. What His birth means for us is no longer that important.

Jesus usually speaks to me clearly each Christmas, and I didn't like what He said this year. He said, "Son, you haven't paid attention to what I spoke through John in Revelation 3:15–18. I know everything you have done, and you are not cold or hot. I wish you were either one or the other. But since you are lukewarm and neither cold not hot, I will spit you out of my mouth.

"You claim to be rich and successful and have everything you need, but you don't know how bad off you are.

"You are pitiful, poor, blind, and naked.

"Buy your gold from me. It has been refined in fire, and it will make you rich. Buy white clothes from me. Wear them, and you can cover up your shameful nakedness. Buy medicine for your eyes so that you will be able to see."

The book of Matthew recounts how God will divide us into His sheep and His goats, and why:

> When the Son of Man comes in His glory (His majesty and splendor), and all the holy angels with Him, then He will sit on the throne of His glory. All nations will be gathered before Him, and He will separate them [the people] from one another as a shepherd separates his sheep from the goats; And He will cause the sheep to stand at His right hand, but the goats at His left. Then the King will say to those at His right hand, Come, you blessed of My Father [you favored of God and appointed to eternal salvation], inherit (receive as your own) the kingdom prepared for you from the foundation of the world. For I was hungry and you gave Me food, I was thirsty and you gave Me something to drink, I was a stranger and you brought Me together with yourselves and welcomed and entertained and lodged Me, I was naked and you clothed Me, I was sick and you visited Me with help and ministering care, I was in prison and you came to see Me. Then the just and upright will answer Him, Lord, when did we see You hungry and gave You food, or thirsty and gave You something to drink? And when did we see You a stranger and welcomed and entertained You, or naked and clothed You? And when did we see You sick or in prison and came to visit You? And the King will reply to them, Truly I tell you, in so far as you did it for one of the least [in the estimation of men] of these My brethren, you did it for Me. Then He will say to those at His left hand, Begone from Me, you cursed, into the eternal fire prepared for the devil and his angels! For I was hungry and you gave Me no food, I was thirsty and you gave Me nothing to drink, I was a stranger and you did not welcome Me and entertain Me, I was naked and you

did not clothe Me, I was sick and in prison and you did not visit Me with help and ministering care. Then they also [in their turn] will answer, Lord, when did we see You hungry or thirsty or a stranger or naked or sick or in prison, and did not minister to You? And He will reply to them, Solemnly I declare to you, in so far as you failed to do it for the least [in the estimation of men] of these, you failed to do it for Me. Then they will go away into eternal punishment, but those who are just and upright and in right standing with God into eternal life. (Matthew 25:31–46)

Surely this is a message for us who call ourselves Christians, asking us to decide whether we are going to get on fire for God and quit being lukewarm, or whether He is going to spit us out of His mouth. Most of the groups that church groups condemn—the gays, the greedy corporations, our politicians who support ungodly causes—know they are cold to God. God is saying that He would rather us be like them than to be lukewarm while professing we are Christians. This Scripture seems to indicate that He is so displeased with the lukewarm that He wants to vomit them out of His stomach. They are contaminating His body.

This may be a good year to look at ourselves and our lukewarm groups that call themselves Christians, misrepresenting Jesus to the world. Just as He said, "Or how can you say to your brother, Brother, allow me to take out the speck that is your eye, when you yourself do not see the beam that is your own eye?" (Luke 6:42). It is time for me to look at the beam in my eye and quit blaming others for my problems and our county's problems. In other words, it is time to clean up our own houses and quit worrying about others.

In Matthew 12:30, Jesus says, "He who is not with Me [definitely on My side] is against Me, and he who does not [definitely] gather with Me and for My side scatters." Is a lukewarm person for Him or against Him?

Jesus didn't come to tell us how to live a good life; He came to heal us from all our spiritual bruises, so we could be like Him and would reflect Him to the world. Then our eyes would be opened to see others through His eyes, and we could be instruments of healing instead of condemnation. God detests lukewarm people.

Maybe people should be lukewarm to the God represented in most or our so-called Christian groups, the groups that tell of Jesus' teaching and how He wants us to live just as the teachers in the temple did in His time. Teaching without the power to back up what is being taught is no more than the law in disguise. The only difference between teachers and Jesus is that He taught and also displayed not only the love of God but also the power of God to back up what He taught. A true Christian group demonstrates the power of Jesus' resurrected blood as it is displayed through His brothers and sisters. A true Christian group brings healing to the brokenhearted and sets captives free.

We all are in need of Jesus' healing. Here are some statistics for the United States: Over 33 percent of American women and over 20 percent of American men have been sexually molested. Over 40 percent of North American women have had abortions, which means, of course, that 40 percent of North American men have also been involved in the murder of a child. That is easily over 50 percent of our population that has suffered molestation or been involved with abortion. Can anyone in this group ever be free to be a mate or parent without being healed and forgiven? We all know the answer is no. Jesus died to heal these people. Without dealing directly with these issues through the power of His resurrected blood and seeing people set free, how can we call ourselves a church representing Jesus? Only the lukewarm could ignore that over half of our population is in need of our help and Jesus' healing.

We have gotten so far off track because lukewarm is the norm in most groups that call themselves Christians. No wonder there are so many divorces: lukewarm relationships!

On Which Side of the Jordan Are the People with Whom You Regularly Meet?

Are the people you regularly meet on the desert side of the Jordan or the Promised Land side? In most of our established institutions, we have been satisfied with living on the wrong side of the Jordan, just trying to be good and trying to claim we are at peace where there is no peace.

The vast majority of churchgoers have developed a false sense of security that misleads them into believing they are members of God's family simply by being members of their churches. Most of those people will probably spend eternity in hell, not heaven. If we lead them to believe that we do not have to each pick up our cross, follow Jesus, and suffer as He suffered, we will most likely end up in hell with them.

Suffering is part of the program, and it takes faith to deal with the giants.

• Rejection • Molestation • Shame • Divorce • Broken and bruised hearts • Calamities that break us down • Being crushed		• Not being loved by a parent • Not being loved by our children • Being sick all the time • Being weak • Feeling unworthy of the good life

The list goes on and on. Even after we join God's family, there are still giants to battle and troubles to face. Satan is coming after us the same way he did Jesus. There are battles to be fought and the joy of victories to be shared.

There will be grumbling and bickering too, as those who resist facing their giants will start all kinds of problems. They have more faith in their bandages and shields of self-righteousness that they have built than they have interest in throwing down their shields and dealing with their spiritual and emotional bruises with the help of Jesus. Unfortunately, this is the problem with so many of our leaders: they are afraid of the giants.

Other leaders have been trained by other seminaries and denominational officials, to try to maintain peace on the wrong side of the Jordan. They are not intentionally doing anything wrong. They are proclaiming peace where there is no peace and endeavoring to maintain their establishments without encountering the wrath of Satan and his army of demons. Satan has given them a good plan:

1. Limit the group's time together to a few hours on one day of the week.

2. Make the groups large, and fill their time together with entertainment so that there is no real fellowship.

3. Preach a sermon, and if the people don't get it, it is not the fault of the preacher or the institution; it is the fault of the people for not listening and obeying.

Satan has designed a good plan to trap people. Consider this: the divorce rate among those who profess to be Christians is the same as the rate for those who don't profess to be Christians. Most churches and church leaders have never crossed the Jordan and will lead you to stay on the wrong side. Your relationships will fail without your trusting Jesus to lead you to defeat the giants and strongholds in your life. This formula leads to failed lives and relationships, which is exactly what Satan wants.

How Deep Is Your Praise?

Several years ago, I was in praise and worship service when the Lord spoke to my heart and said, "The person behind you is praising me at a much deeper level than the rest of you." I looked behind me and to the side and saw a good friend of mine, Gary Peters. Then I saw the woman behind me and realized it was she whom God was speaking about. God said, "She has been healed of much more than the rest of you. The rest of the group's praises are really shallow in comparison to hers."

Back in the denominational church, it seemed that the people were just repeating words. They even hired professional musicians to lead their music and make it better.

There was no life in the music because there was no life in the choir singers. Now so many church groups brought in new live music, which sounds better, but it has no real life unless the musicians and singers are singing to Jesus with their hearts because of the things He has done in their lives.

When I was in prison in Big Springs, Texas, a man came in who was a classical pianist; he could play all the notes, and they sounded great.

He found Jesus and the power of the Holy Spirit, and his music changed. He led us into the presence of the God he knew. He was playing for God, not an audience.

Over the years, I have learned that most of us are actually angry with God deep down inside. We have thought, *God, if you are so good, why didn't you stop that person from hurting me? God, if you are so good, why didn't you make this or that happen in my life?* We could make a list so long that a thousand pages would not be enough. Because we have been taught that God is perfect and we can't be angry with Him, we pretend we aren't.

We can't fool Him, though. He knows we are angry with Him, even when we act like we aren't. When you are angry with someone, you can be nice to his face and even sing songs to him. Deep down inside, you are not going to let him close to you.

As parents, we would rather our children come confront us with their anger so that we can rebuild the bridge between us. We want close fellowship with our children, and so does God. Several years ago, God spoke to me and said, "People are angry with me for something I let happen or didn't make happen. I want you to quit trying to answer their questions for me. I am a big boy; let me answer them for myself. I am at the door, knocking with tears in my eyes, waiting for them to let me in so I can sit down, talk with them, and bring them truth and healing. Then and only then will their praise and worship become deep and real."

As the He says in Scripture, "If My people, who are called by My name, shall humble themselves, pray, *seek, crave, and require of necessity My face* and turn from their wicked ways, then will I hear from heaven, forgive their sin, and heal their land" (2 Chronicles 7:14, emphasis added). We have to need Him urgently, to require out of necessity His face, if we want to be healed, turn from our wicked ways, and actually love God and others.

The Parable of the College Football Team

Let's say that I have been hired to be the athletic director of a college, and my first assignment is to form a college football team. The first thing I need to do is hire coaches, all of whom must have advanced degrees. I will require a doctorate for the head coach, and all his assistants will need to have master's degrees.

Experience playing football will not be a requirement, but it is helpful.

In order to attract good recruits, we will need to build nice facilities.

Upon finding our recruits, we will schedule classes for them once per week. They will spend one hour with an assistant coach and one hour with the head coach.

In class, the assistants will give the players their playbooks. However, on our team, you do not have to study or complete the homework to stay on the team. There are no formal exercise requirements, but players can exercise on their own if they want.

The coaches are busy with more important matters.

There will be no scrimmages, because someone may get hurt, and the coaches do not have the time or expertise to help those who are injured.

It is finally time for the first game against the University of Florida.,

Most of the players show up, but they do not have any padding under their uniforms or helmets for protection. The coaches sit in the stands to see how the players are going to do.

You guessed it: the team comes back to their regular classes all beaten up and discouraged. The coaches just can't understand why the team played so poorly. They give the players another lesson and point fingers at the players for the team's failure. After all, the coaches have taught the team all the coaches know about football. The team keeps getting clobbered, however, with no relief in sight.

As the school's athletic director, I am ultimately responsible for the coaches and the team's failure. I call the coaches in to see what can be done, as attendance and revenues are down. We come up with a great plan: we will give up on winning football games, and, in fact, we will forget about football all together. We will concentrate on pep rallies. We will hire inspirational speakers, improve the music, and add some new programs. We will judge our success or failure by how many people show up to the pep rallies and how much money they contribute.

We have given up on God's game, His plan for victory through the cross and through His blood. Jesus not only teaches His players; He takes His players onto the field with Him. A teacher and trainer, He uses an effective teaching method called individual discipleship.

Ephesians 4 says that our leaders are to equip us to do the work of ministering. Teaching and preaching have failed because they are only part of leadership. All leaders are judged by what their followers are doing. God's real leaders are people like Caleb, people who believe that God gives victory. They concentrate on their mission: salvation here on earth, healing the brokenhearted, and setting the captives free through the power of the resurrected blood of Jesus. Through their leadership, Jesus' good news spreads and people want to join Jesus' team.

It is time to get rid of the athletic directors and the coaches who are not leading us to victory in our Promised Land.

Churches or groups that claim to represent Christ are supposed to be hospitals for the hurting. No intelligent person would keep going to a hospital or doctor without ever getting healed. Maybe the hospitals and doctors are the problem—not the patients who don't return.

Seek First the Kingdom of God and His Righteousness

Scripture tells us not to worry about what we are going to eat, drink, or wear. "For the Gentiles (heathen) wish for and crave and diligently seek all these things, and your heavenly Father knows well that you need them all. But seek (aim at and strive after) first of all His Kingdom and His righteousness (His way of doing and being right), and then all these things taken together will be given you besides" (Matthew 6:31–33).

When I first read these verses, their message seemed like a big task for someone like me who had worried and strived for things all my life. My first trial came very soon after entering the prison gates. During the first year, a prisoner was allowed to have a jogging suit. I had the best-looking suit on the compound. After getting off from washing pots and pans, I would take a shower, put that suit on, and strut around the recreation yard.

One day I felt the Lord was telling me to give the suit to this man who had no front teeth. After a few days, I gave in and took it to him. I told him I didn't want to give it to him, but the Lord was forcing my hand. I got back to my bunk, and lying on the bed was a version of the Bible I had wanted. The Lord spoke through that inner voice, saying, "This is what you need."

I felt that He was telling me to give away everything I made, all of the fifteen dollars per month I earned washing pots and pans, and He told me to give away half of what people gave me. My thought was, *Lord, you must be crazy*. I know it isn't good to put out a fleece to determine His will. I was a very young Christian, so He accommodated me. I am not a basketball player; football was my game. I stood at the top of the key and said, "Lord, if this is you, let me ring the next three baskets." I knew I was safe because there was no way I could make three baskets in a row. I was wrong, and all three balls went swish in the net.

I thought, *Here we go, Lord*. I didn't have anyone on the outside sending me money. The previous night, I had read the Scripture about seeking first the kingdom of God and had written that verse, Matthew 6:33, on a piece of paper in my pocket.

That Saturday, on the way back from breakfast, an officer stopped me and said I had a letter. It was from Melissa Doyle, a young girl whose family was very poor at the time. There was a yellow slip inside, indicating that she had sent me a dollar. I could go to the commissary that week, and I was going to buy a bottle of shampoo for seventy-five cents and wanted to buy a bar of Tone soap for fifty cents. I was twenty-five cents short, so I bought a hotel bar of Zest for a quarter instead. I went to the barbershop, borrowed an empty bottle, and poured half of the shampoo into it. Then I said, "Lord, what do you want me to do with this soap?" He told me to give it away, and so I did. No one knew what I had done but me. The next day, an inmate walked up to me out of the blue and handed me a bag with two bars of Tone soap, toothpaste, and razors inside. I will never forget that day.

I don't have time to tell about all the supernatural things that happened that year, but here is another. I saw a program on TV about a men's ministry. I wanted to write them, but I didn't have a stamp. I wrote the letter anyway. That night, I was walking off the recreation yard and Doc, a fellow inmate, turned to me and said, "For some reason, I feel like the Lord is telling me to give you one stamp."

The year before I was released from prison, I spent time in the prison in Big Springs, Texas. I felt the Lord was telling me to make out a budget, and He would supply the money. I had a job that paid thirty-two dollars per month, so that is what I made my budget for. He told me to add some ice cream and other things I would never have bought. He said, "Go ahead; I will look after you." I filled it out for forty dollars, not knowing where the eight dollars would come from.

That night, my roommate came in and said, "I sold a pair of tennis shoes today. I was walking back from my job and asked the Lord what He wanted me to do with the money. He said, 'Give Billy eight dollars.' Well, then I said, 'Lord, Billy has money. Why should I give it to him?'" My roommate said the Lord just repeated that he was to give me the eight dollars. He did, and the Lord came through just as He said He would. He was preparing me for a much larger test.

When I got out of prison, I received two letters from the IRS. One was a bill for $999,999; the other was a bill for $80,001. The letters said to send the money by return mail. I had left prison with $124 to my name and was only making $200 per week. The Lord said, "Do not worry about it; you really do not owe this much. Someone has just blamed his or her problems on you." I ended up settling for $7,500, and someone else paid it.

I believe if we work for God, if we aim at and strive after, first of all, His kingdom and His righteousness (His ways of doing and being right), all these things—forgiveness, sustenance, and a bit extra—will be given to us.

We experience real and right relationships when we trust our deepest bruises and pleasures with God and when we are aware of those things that are not from Him. We must sit down and open the door for Him to come in and talk to us about anything He wants to.

If a man is on BJ Construction's payroll but decides to work this week for Regional Construction, it is not up to BJ Construction to pay him. If we are not on God's job, it is not His responsibility to look after us. I know I have gotten off His job and ended up in trouble before. Relationships will not last long unless we have a right relationship with God. Seeking the things of this world first will destroy our lives and families, so we must stay on God's job and seek His kingdom first.

How Do God's Reward Plan and Satan's Punishment Plan Work?

Do we really care for our loved ones and for those who have already left this life? How can we learn from God's reward plan us for us, and how can we learn from Satan's, in order to make choices that bring others and ourselves rewards instead of punishments?

The Bible tells us, "But without faith it is impossible to please and be satisfactory to Him. For whoever would come near to God must [necessarily] believe that God exists and that He is a rewarder of those who earnestly and diligently seek Him [out]" (Hebrews 11:6). And in Genesis 22:17, God speaks to Abraham about His reward plan: "In blessing I will bless you and in multiplying I will multiply your descendants like the stars to the heavens and like the sand on the seashore.

"And your Seed (Heir) will possess the gate of His enemies." As far as I can tell, Abraham only had two sons, Ishmael and Isaac. Abraham conceived Ishmael with Hagar when he and Sarah were trying desperately to bring about God's reward of a son. Isaac was conceived God's way in God's timing, and Isaac became Abraham's heir. Isaac was born because of Abraham's faith.

Also because of Abraham's faith, his descendants through Isaac are uncountable. Abraham is rewarded every time someone comes into the kingdom of God. Jesus is rewarded every time someone comes into the kingdom with a new brother or sister or friend. God's reward plan is for all of us. The faith we share on earth will be rewarded for generations to come. However, the reward is contingent upon what others on earth do with their faith. God's reward plan is like a multi-level marketing plan. The reward grows as the number of faithful increases. The plan rewards us for those we bring into the kingdom and for those in whom we plant seeds. The people we come in contact with every day give us opportunities to increase our eternal reward. If we pass by these opportunities, we cut back on our reward as well as the rewards for those who have positively impacted our faith. If we love God, those who have gone before us, and ourselves, we will be yoked with Jesus and led by Him to work in His harvest.

Hebrews 11 gives us the names of a group of people who had great faith: Abraham, Isaac, Jacob, Joseph, Moses, Rahab, Gideon, Barak, Sampson, Jephtha, David, Samuel, and others who suffered the trials of mocking, scourging, and even imprisonment. Others were "sawn asunder," slaughtered, destitute, oppressed, and cruelly treated. The Bible goes on to tell us that:

> all of these, though they won divine approval by [means
> of] their faith, did not receive the fulfillment of what was
> promised, because God had us in mind and had something

better and greater in view for us, so that they [those heroes and heroines of faith] should not come to perfection apart from us [before we join them]. Therefore, then, since we are surrounded by so great a cloud of witnesses [who have borne testimony to the Truth] let us strip off and throw aside every encumbrance (unnecessary weight) and that sin which so readily (deftly and cleverly) clings to and entangles us, and let us run with patient endurance and steady and active persistence the appointed course of the race that is set before us. (Hebrews 11:39–12:1)

The plan works for those who have gone before us, whether they are in heaven or hell.

In heaven, everyone will thank and be thankful for those who went before and those who come after them. In hell, everyone will blame and scream at everyone who went before and those who come after them.

Heaven is a place of rewards, and hell is a place of punishment. The structure is the same, though the spirit, of course, is different: thanking versus cursing, reward versus punishment, and so on.

In Genesis 3, Adam blamed God and Eve for his sin, and Eve blamed the serpent. They were banished from the Promised Land forever.

Matthew 16 tells the a story of a rich man and a poor beggar named Lazarus, who was brought to the rich man's house.

Lazarus was happy just to eat the scraps that fell from the rich man's table. His body was covered with sores, which dogs kept coming up to lick. When Lazarus died, angels took him to the place of honor next to Abraham. When the rich man died and was buried, he went to hell and suffered terribly. When the rich man looked up and saw Abraham far off with Lazarus at his side, he said, "Abraham, have pity on me! Send Lazarus to dip his finger in water and touch my tongue. I'm suffering terribly in this fire." Abraham answered, "My friend, remember that while you lived, you had everything good, and Lazarus had everything bad. Now he is happy, and you are in pain. And besides, there is a deep ditch between us, and no one from either side can cross over."

The rich man then said, "Abraham, then, please send Lazarus to my father's home. Let him warn my five brothers, so they won't come to this horrible place."

The rich man probably didn't want his brothers to come down there for two reasons: first, so they wouldn't suffer, and second, so they would not increase his torment. We choose what we do with our time and our money to encourage others in the direction of reward or torment.

Let me give you an example using a person's estate. Perhaps the estate is left in the hands of someone who is going to invest her time and the money to build up the kingdom of God. If the person leaving the estate goes to heaven, the person leaving the estate will see an increased reward. If the person goes to hell, his torment will be decreased because the estate manager is working for the kingdom.

If the estate is left to someone who doesn't use the estate to increase the kingdom of God, there will be no reward for the one who left the estate. If someone goes to hell and leaves their estate to someone who is not using it for God's kingdom, their punishment will increase.

Everything set before us is an opportunity for reward or punishment for ourselves and for those who come before and after us.

We can cry and mourn for those who pass before us. Whether we really love them or not will be made clear by what we do with the rest of our lives. Our love is not reflected by what we say or how we act at the funeral and immediately afterward.

The rewards of a relationship with God are not only fulfilled on earth. They can be passed on to those who have gone before you and the ones coming after. Here is some of what Scripture says about God's reward:

> For the son of Man is going to come in the glory (majesty, splendor) of His father with His angels, and then He will render account and reward every man in accordance with what he has done. (Matthew 16:27)

> And all the assemblies (churches) shall recognize and understand that I am He Who searches minds (the thoughts, feelings, and purposes) and the [inmost] hearts, and I will give to each of you [the reward for what you have done] as your work deserves. (Revelation 11:18)

> Behold, I am coming soon, and I shall bring My wages
> and rewards with me, to repay and render to each one just
> what his own actions and work merit. (Revelation 22:1)

What are you going to do with the rest of your life? Do you really love your family? Do you really love those who have died before you? Do you really love yourself? Who are you going to leave your estate to?

It Is Never Too Late for Older People to Believe

When I was taking my daddy to the doctor in the latter years of his life, I would hear older people talking about and wondering whether they were saved and going to heaven. I believe older people who have been attending churches where the power of the resurrection is not on display are seeking the truth about the most important matter in their lives. We do not need to give up on them. My daddy, who believed that he had given enough money to the Methodist Church that he had bought his right to go to heaven, accepted the Living Savior the year before he died. My mother, who believed as a Methodist that she could believe the parts of the Bible she wanted to and what she wanted to about those parts, took the time to study a little. She accepted Christ in her late seventies.

Here is the testimony of another older person who is in the latter days and weeks of his life. His heart is so damaged that the doctors don't give him much time.

> My name is Kenneth; I've been here in this institution fifteen and a half years. I have been a Christian since 1991. At least that was the year I accepted Jesus into my life. I had peace within myself knowing that the Lord had forgiven all my sins at the cross and that I no longer was in danger of an eternal hell. I called upon the name of Jesus to come into my life and save me. He said, "For whosoever shall call upon the Lord shall be saved"

(Romans 10:13). And He is faithful to His word (1 John 1:9). Yes, I had peace, but no joy or fellowship with my Savior, Jesus Christ. And I became angry towards God because I wasn't getting what I expected to receive. And for sixty-plus years I lived my life full of anger and doubt. I am now seventy-four years old, and I have only come to know the truth in the past month.

Here I was, seventy-four years old, had read the Bible cover to cover over a dozen times, and had also done deep studies of His word and ways. Yet I still had no joy, nor felt an honest relationship with God. Why? Yes, I was saved, so why did I not have the joy and fellowship that others seemed to have? People were walking around with a smile on their faces, although they were doing life in prison, some with a dozen life sentences. Were they suffering insanity? No. They had Jesus in their hearts, and they had a relationship with their God. So I started going to the chapel to services, I started going with "Kairos." Then the Lord opened my mind and heart to know the meaning of fellowship.

I went to Kairos and was greatly impressed with the fellowship they showed. I then signed up for Celebrate Recovery, and what an eye-opener it has been. I began to learn about myself, and to know that without fully trusting in Jesus, I was living in darkness. And for most of my seventy-four years on this earth, I have been separated from Christ because I never gave Him all my dirty baggage. Although I was saved, I was still living my life in darkness, ashamed of my past sins, my unforgiving heart, hate, lust, covetousness, and on and on walls of separation I had built for sixty-five years of my life, even up to a month ago.

Then God started dealing with me in my second week in Recovery by listening to others share their hang-ups, opening up to each other, trusting in each other. I had to face my denial. I was keeping all my emotions bottled up inside me, all the hurts I had done to others for sixty-five years, all the hurts that were done to me. But all the hurts I caused far outweighed the hurts caused by others to me. My life was out of control.

By sharing my inner emotions and really looking to God to heal me, I began to trust another human being. That person was the volunteer, our Recovery sponsor. We went into a private room and had a one-on-one talk. I told him of my past sins and how I've lived with not being able to forgive myself. But what I was in fact saying (without realizing it) was that I was not trusting God to heal me of these things I couldn't forgive myself for. I hated the condition I was in spiritually. We never finished our talk till three weeks later. When we came together again, he told me the reason I wasn't healed years ago was I never gave it all to Jesus. He said Jesus never did leave me, that He has been waiting for me to come to Him and lay all my hang-ups and sorrows that life brings to me at the foot of His cross and leave it there. He would take them and He would heal me.

Brother Billy said, "Let's pray." When I started praying, the strangest thing happened. My body, from the top of my head to the bottom of my feet, started tingling—goose bumps. And tears started flowing from my eyes that I couldn't stop, nor did I want to. Not tears of hurt or sorrow, but for the first time in my seventy-four years I was filled with joy. I felt the Lord's presence all around me and in me. I also heard the voice of God. He said, "All these wasted years you have locked Me out from healing you. The door has been opened and you invited Me in to heal you. And My word is true. You are healed because of your faith and trust in Me. Now I can give you the blessings I've always had for you." That was all I heard. I thanked Him for healing me. The prayer ended but the tears didn't. In all my seventy-four years I've never felt the peace and joy that came over me. I knew that the Lord had set me free. Now I could have the relationship I had been searching for.

You see, God is real, Jesus is real, and the Holy Spirit is real. And once I turned everything over to my Higher Power, Jesus, then I also was real in my relationship with God. No, I am not perfect, and I know I will never be as long as I am in this body of flesh. However, I also know that from here on I no longer have to carry around any hang-ups I will come across. I'll just give them to Jesus, and He can handle them. God gave me an accountability partner, one that I can go to and share my innermost feelings with, good and bad. I trust him, Bro. Steven is someone I can talk to. The Lord gave him to me. So I know that I can put my trust in him. God healed him, so he is able to encourage me. He is no better than I am; he is just stronger in his relationship with God. But I'm growing each moment of my life now. And through this Recovery program, and with prayer and study of His written word, I now have an everlasting relationship with my God.

I've been in prison forty-five years now, and I may never be set free from this prison (which is also in God's hands). But my God has healed my wounded body and has set me free, so I can now be used for His glory. It's no longer about me, but about Him and His will for me. Today He will also set you free and heal you. You only have to invite Him to come in, and He will come in. No matter what kind of sins or hang-ups you may have in your life, He will heal you.

In closing my testimony, I want to leave this with you— James 1:12–24. We all would do well to consider what God is telling us.

The joy and peace be upon all who trust Him.

Kenneth

Today is no time to think we are doing good by appease those older people until they die. It is time to bring truth and healing that will last for eternity.

It is Not to Late for Older People to Change the World

Younger people listen a lot more to older people than you think. I hear younger people all the time quoting from their parents and grandparents, good and bad. Don't give up on younger people; we have a lot to offer and plant truth into them. I just explained fasting to my nine-year-old granddaughter. She listened and understood. She just tested me by baking a pan of chocolatechip cookies; she put one in my face and said, "You can't have one," as my stomach was growling. The Bible says the older people are to minister to the younger people. Young couples and single parents really need us to reach out to them as they are struggling in this fast-paced world, and for the most part, believe things can solve their problems.

Here is a plan that cannot fail for older people. If one older person would get the first names of a school class and commit to pray for those twenty or so students by name for thirty minutes a day while school is in session, what a difference it would make in the students and the person praying.

- Twenty people who got together would be praying for over four hundred students.

- Fifty would be praying for over a thousand students.

- Two hundred would be praying for over four thousand students.

The numbers are staggering.

One person with a vision could change an entire community of children. Not a preacher of a church, because the vision needs to be for a community not limited to church or denomination. It is easier for lay people than the preacher to come together.

Here is a strategy for the visionary.

- The army should be retired people. There is no reason a retired person cannot give up thirty minutes a day for children and for Christ.

- Find a person in an organization such as a church group or civic organization to buy in to the vision and get written commitments from the people and post the goal for the community, just as the united fund does each year in very visible places in the community.

- The individual commitments should be in writing.

- The first names of the students should be obtained by a student in the class, not going to the school system or their employees.

- The name of the teacher should be obtained, and if led by the Holy Spirit, contacted letting them know they are being prayed for. If there is a special need, they can contact you.

I will be sixty-nine in November, and we older people can still change the world for generations to come if we will come together with a vision and strategy. You might want to start by inviting a young couple over for a meal once a month or offering to babysit for them.

Forgiveness Is a Process

Confess. Seek God's face. Accept His truth. Accept responsibility for the ones you hurt out of your pain. Repent. Accept new life in Jesus and share what God has done for you with others. Forgiveness, in other words, is a process.

Saying you want to forgive someone is the first step in the forgiveness process. Until the bruise is healed, however, true forgiveness has not taken place. In order for Jesus to heal our bruises, we need to take up our crosses and follow Him. Jesus will not wipe away our memories; He will take the pain out of our memories. We all hurt others out of our own bruises, so we have to be ready to ask forgiveness for those we have hurt.

Jesus said to confess our sins to one another so that we may be healed. We usually try to bury our pain and think we have forgiven our offenders. Jesus' way is to deal directly with the pain.

When you take your pain to the cross, you will feel and suffer that pain like it is happening all over again. Then, if you open the door and invite Jesus into the pain, He will bring you truth and healing. When Jesus went to the cross, He did His part. It was then up to the Father and the Holy Spirit to resurrect Him. When we take our pain to the cross and invite Jesus in, we have done our part. God will then do His part. The pain will be resurrected in peace, joy, and forgiveness to bring us closer to our mates and others. Try to begin the forgiveness process, and Jesus will show up. He died for this. You will come face to face with Him.

Which Side of the Cross-Are You Ministering From?

Are you ministering from the suffering side of the cross or the resurrected side? If you are ministering out of the suffering side of your life that has not been resurrected, you are ministering death instead of life. It is so easy for us to sympathize with or judge hurting people when we are still hurting. It is another matter altogether to bring life and hope to someone who is hurting, because you have been healed through the power of His blood.

So many hurting people are attracted to the prison ministry because they want to share their pain. It is if they are stuck in their pain and want someone to share it with them. As Christians, we can be sympathetic and feel their pain, but we must call on Jesus' resurrected blood to bring life and stop the suffering.

Some people are in love with their pain and love to sit down and share it with everyone. This is called a pity party. Jesus is not in the pity party business. He is in the resurrection, life, peace, and joy business.

I used to be really zealous, wanting to go out and minister and even start my own ministries, without realizing that I first needed a lot more dying and resurrecting in me before I was ready to lead a public ministry. Marriage is God's best refining tool. I needed to learn how to rule, or love, in my family before becoming a Christian leader; 1 Timothy 4 is clear on this point. In the last five or six years, I have started working on the big project, the project of myself, and have let God start to change me. That change is reflected in my relationship with my wife Cissy.

Finally, after more than twenty-seven years, I am prepared. My journey would have been a lot shorter if I had been more concerned about picking up my cross daily and finding my resurrection, my new life in Christ, sooner.

We Need to Take Our
Treasures to the Cross

Our treasures, such as our house, cars, TV, and relationships, may not all look so good through the eyes of the cross.

We have a tendency to only take the things we think are bad to the cross for examination through Jesus' eyes. We have to take everything to Jesus to find out the truth, as He is the only one who knows the truth about what is best for our lives and us. Whether it is idolizing or abusing children, becoming successful in business, or having a bigger house and newer cars, all these can lead to destruction.

Trying to have a relationship with your partner will not work while you are remembering that old girlfriend or boyfriend or holding on to your mother and daddy (or having them hold on to you) instead of becoming one with your spouse. And the list goes on.

The things we think are good can destroy us and those around us.

Do You Understand the Prayer That Jesus Taught Us to Pray?

What is the reason Satan and his followers are running wild on earth? Can it be that we don't understand the power God has vested in us to defeat Satan? As documented in Luke 11:2–4, Jesus taught us to pray a powerful prayer that is important to understand.

Our Father in Heaven, Hallowed Be Your Name

Before starting a conversation, it helps to know something about the person we're talking with and our relationship to her. Can she hear us? Does she want to speak? If the person is a stranger, we would not talk as we would to family. We'd talk differently with a relative who was stern and judgmental than we would to one who was kind, gentle, caring, and who always wanted the best for us. All conversations are controlled by our relationship with the person we are speaking with and what we believe about that person.

If we have accepted Jesus as Lord of our lives, we have been adopted by God the Father, who is kind, gentle, caring, and always wants the best for us and everyone else (Galatians 4:6). He is in heaven and loves to sit down and have talks with us. He has adopted us and given us His name, a name we must proclaim with pride. We are sons and daughters of the King of Kings. We are princes and princesses with crowns on our heads and with the right to proclaim to the world who we are and to whom we belong.

We should be proud of our Papa and want to tell everyone about Him. Jesus said, "Let your light shine before men in such a way that they see your good works, and glorify your Father, who is in heaven" (Matthew 6:16). People will know who we represent by what we say, what we do, and how we act.

Your Kingdom Come, Your Will Be Done, on Earth as it Is in Heaven

God the Father seated Jesus at His right hand in heavenly places "far above all rule and authority and power and dominion and every name that is named [above every title that can be conferred], not only in this age and in this world, but also in the age and the world which are to come" (Ephesians 1:20–21). As our eyes are opened (Luke 4:18), we will come to see that we have joint seating with Jesus in heavenly places "For he raised us from the dead along *with* Christ and *seated* us *with him* in the heavenly realms because we are *united with* Christ Jesus" (Ephesians 2:6–7 NLT, emphasis added). It is our Father's desire that we see and understand our inheritance, the immeasurable, unlimited, and surpassing greatness of His power in and for us who believe, as demonstrated in His mighty strength (Ephesians 1:18–19).

Now that we know who we are and whose family we are part of, we are ready to go about bringing His kingdom to earth as it is in heaven. We are seated with Jesus, next to our Father. It is like having joint signature authority on a checking account to make transactions in His name. We are His representatives on earth. His plan is for His kingdom to come into existence on earth, just as it is in heaven, and this plan depends on the princes and princesses whom He has given authority to rule and love in His name, with the assistance and power of the Holy Spirit.

Give Us Day by Day Our Daily Bread

The real bread is Jesus (John 6:35). He said, "Do not worry saying, 'What shall we eat?' or 'What shall we drink?' or 'What will we wear?'

"For after all these things the Gentiles seek. For your heavenly Father knows that you need all these things. But seek first the kingdom of God and His righteousness, and all these things shall be added to you" (Matthew 6:31–33). If we are carrying on a conversation with God and seeking His kingdom, we are in the right relationship with Him. We don't need to be concerned about natural bread. Now all we need to do is to listen to His words after we have given Him the right place in our hearts for us to rule and reign for Him as He has assigned us.

Have you ever worked for someone? Did you have to beg him to tell you what he wanted you to do? No.

Why is it so hard for us to understand that God wants to talk to us? He wants us to be fully present with Him each day. As He said, "Therefore, do not worry about tomorrow, for tomorrow will worry about its own things. Sufficient for the day is its own trouble. If we are about today's words (bread) tomorrow will take care of itself" (Matthew 6:34).

When Jesus died on the cross, the curtain to the Holy of Holies was ripped open so we could all approach God twenty-four/seven (Mark 15:18). We no longer have any excuses for not visiting with Him daily or for not knowing His will. Now all we have to do is listen (His words, our bread) and obey to work with Him to bring His kingdom to earth. As He works through us, our enemies will become footstools for our feet.

Forgive Us Our Sins, for We Also Forgive Everyone Who Is Indebted to Us

As it says in Matthew 6:14–15, "For if you forgive others for their transgressions, your heavenly Father will also forgive you. But if you do not forgive others, then your Father will not forgive your transgressions."

There are several ways to look at "forgive us of our sins," and many of us have missed the mark in our interpretations. Most of us have believed that this references the things we have done wrong in our lives. Yes, it does, but maybe there is a much deeper meaning also. *Webster's Dictionary* says sin is "an offense against God." Is it an offense against God when we don't trust Him enough to do what He has asked us to do? Is it an offense when we are ashamed of Him and don't brag about Him to others? Is it an offense when we ignore Him and don't even want to visit with Him? How would you like it if your children lived next door, but if instead of coming to visit regularly, they went to a building to hear someone speak about a book you wrote? Alternatively, what if they just read the book occasionally? God probably feels like you would feel: deeply hurt.

Let me give you a practical example of not caring or obeying. Let's say I am in the roofing business, and we are re-roofing the home you love. We have torn off all the shingles and the felt, leaving the house exposed to the elements. You go out of town for a few hours. While driving back, you hear a warning signal on the radio that a severe rainstorm is in your area. The sky confirms the broadcast; the clouds are dark.

As you ride by, you notice our trucks at the bar. You stop and ask us if we've covered your roof. We say, "No, we're just taking a couple of hours for lunch; your house will be okay. We'll be back in an hour or so." You try to explain that it's going to storm. I say, "Don't worry. There are people you can hire to fix the house from the rain damage." Are you going to be more upset because we are at the bar drinking or because your house is about to be ruined and we don't care enough to protect it? We all know the answer. You'll be upset about your home and the fact that we don't care anything about it.

This is most likely the way God sees sin. Sin is not so much about what we are doing wrong; our biggest sin is that we don't care enough about Him to protect His house and the people in it. If we had been working on the roof, we couldn't have been at the bar. There is a battle for His kingdom to come. It's not just a matter of what we *don't do.* He actually expects us to follow His instructions, storming the gates of hell and bringing His family, His kingdom, to earth as it is in heaven.

After our eyes are open, we will see what ungrateful sinners we are. It will be easy to forgive others. It is our own self-righteousness that hurts us. If we don't forgive others, we haven't looked at all the self-righteous acts that have caused so much pain to others. Until we are willing to look into the mirror and see what sinners we are, we really don't know Him. Without forgiving hearts, we have never accepted Him as our Lord.

Do Not Lead Us into Temptation, but Deliver Us from Evil

God will not lead us into any temptation that He has not prepared us to overcome. Most of our temptations come from our evil desires. Our problem is that we aren't listening to Him in order to prepare for the temptations our enemy has prepared for us. God will deliver us from evil as we call upon Him and listen for His path.

We can't just study a book and learn about God, although studying the Bible is very important.

The Bible is God's direction, His love letter, and His words, but it's not God. Just listening to someone preach and teach won't do the job either. Jesus said, "Take my yoke upon you and learn from Me, for I am gentle and humble in heart, and *you will* find rest for your souls" (Matthew 11:29, emphasis added). When we find rest, we have something to share with others that they will want to hear. There is no other way than spending time alone with Him, listening, walking with Him, and then trusting and obeying Him.

Why is Satan's kingdom running wild on earth? Is it that we have not found rest for our souls? Can it be that we don't understand who we are? Is it that we don't love others enough to use the power and authority we have been given, seated next to Jesus, to get free and then bring that hope to others, so that they can find freedom and rest? There is a problem in the formula somewhere, because Satan has not become a footstool. Either Jesus is a liar and we need to give up all this foolishness or we are the problem.

Please take this to your spiritual leader and organize a game plan for victory in Jesus.

We Are Living in Some Very Troubling Times

We live in a country that is financially and spiritually bankrupt, where people bow down to the dollar bill instead of to the cross.

Financial Bankruptcy

A person is bankrupt when she doesn't have the ability to pay her bills; her spending or spending needs outpace her income and her ability to produce income. Her liabilities are larger than her assets.

I saw a news report yesterday on Fox News that said America is borrowing forty-one cents of every dollar the government is spending this year.

Since 1971, the United States has not had any restraints on how much currency it can print. In the thirty-four years prior to 1971, the money supply had increased just twice. Since that time, the supply has increased thirteen times—that is, before the last printings.

Here is a picture of the United States: a family's income goes down because the father loses his good job; his health has deteriorated, and he no longer can produce as he once could. Instead of the family cutting back on expenses, they increase spending and continue buying things they can't afford. They just keep getting more credit cards and running up their debts. How long will it be before the creditors cut them off? In 1971, the United States had a balanced trade with other countries. Since that time, we have been consuming much more than we are producing. We are like a company that is losing business and money and yet goes to the bank to write itself loans without any collateral. With China alone, we are buying one hundred dollars worth of goods, selling them twenty-five dollars worth of goods, and asking them to take notes whose value is inflated for the seventy-five-dollar difference. We have a trade deficit with all of our top twenty trading partners.

Every transaction is based on bartering. I give you something of value for something you have that I want. We are no longer producing more than we are consuming, so what do we have of value to barter with other countries in order to keep obtaining their goods?

Look at our foreign aid. We are giving away money we have borrowed from other countries, and we have no intention or ability to pay it back. Is our foreign aid the United States' foreign aid or China's? How long do you think they are going to put up with us giving their money away?

We are a country that no longer has the desire or ability to pay our debts.

The stimulus package is no more helpful than a man getting a ten-dollar-per-hour job who has recently lost his forty-dollar-per-hour job. He can't pay his bills, and his house is in foreclosure. Someone sends him a credit card with a limit of fifty thousand dollars, and he uses it to pay his bills. That is a picture of the stimulus package.

"THE MCGRUDER CORPORATION IS GOING DOWN THE TUBE. THEY JUST FIRED ME."

It is not a matter of *whether* we are going to have a crash much worse than the one in 1929. It is a matter of *when,* and the time is not far off.

Spiritual Bankruptcy

If you went into 98 percent of the groups (churches) that call themselves Christian in the United States and asked everyone to come forward who could name the person they had led to Christ and tried to disciple in the last five years, what percentage of people in these groups would come forward and share even one name? Five percent would probably be a high number. Remember, "He who is not with Me [definitely on My side] is against Me, and he who does not [definitely] gather with Me and for My side scatters" (Matthew 12:30).

So, then, are the 95 percent of scattering churchgoers for Him or against Him? We all know the answer is *against.* If the group is made up predominantly of those who scatter, whose side is the group on, God's or Satan's? If someone gives money to a group of people who scatter, whose kingdom is she financing?

We have the ability to bring ourselves out of spiritual bankruptcy. If we don't, we are going to have very serious problems when the financial hammer falls, and it is going to fall. To bring yourself out of spiritual bankruptcy, repent, seek God with all your heart, find a leader who is yoked to Jesus (and run from leaders who are not), learn to hear from God, and spend time with others who are seeking and hearing from Him.

You know the crash is coming. You have a choice to be one of the bridesmaids who didn't have enough oil for her lamp until the special day came or one who had stored up an abundance of oil and was prepared.

You have a choice to bury your head in the sand and believe everything will be all right or get prepared with the only one who can carry you through the storm.

We are all part of the problem or part of the solution to healing our land. What are you going to do with the rest of your life? Keep living with your bruises and lies, passing them on to your family and others for generations? Or will you choose to find and live life through the resurrected blood of Jesus?

If we are going to save our country, those of us who are Christians have to start fighting spiritually. We have to have some leaders step up and give us a strategy and start fighting, rather than passively standing by watching our country go down the tubes. Satan and his army have strategies and plans, and they are serious about their business. Where are our leaders and what is our war plan?

You can be healed and set free (if and) when you are willing to invite Jesus in and give up your hang ups and spiritual bruises.

Here is a picture of how I see God's kingdom working

God the Father is the power plant, the source of all power and true knowledge

Jesus is our line to the power plant

The switch releases the power; we control the switch.

When the switch is turned on the power is released.

God's power is the Holy Spirit who brings truth and light into darkness.

There are many "memory rooms" in each of us and we can go back to those rooms. When we go back to those memories we can see and feel what is in that room.

After we go back to a specific room, we turn on the light switch by inviting Jesus into that room. He will come in and all His power and light will show you the truth of how that memory really looks. Then you will know the truth that can set you free. As he reveals the truth of how that room looks, His truth of what happened there, you then have a choice to hold on to your old "furniture" or get rid of it and replace it with His. That is your choice. He died to heal us and is crying out for you to let him in your memory rooms.

Revelation 3:20, "Behold, I stand at the door and knock; if anyone hears and listens to and heeds My voice and opens the door, I will com in to him and will eat with him, and he [will eat] with me.

2 Chronicles 7:14, "If my people, who are called by my name, shall humble themselves, pray, seek, crave, and require of necessity My face and turn from their wicked ways, them will I hear from heaven, forgive their sin, and heal their land.

1 John 1:9, "If we [freely] admit that we have sinned and confess our sins, He is faithful and just (true to His own nature and promises) and will forgive our sins [dismiss our lawlessness] and [continually] cleans us from all unrighteousness [everything not in conformity to His will in purpose, thought and action].

It is simple. Tell someone about the room- confession. Close your eyes and go back to the memory, and when you are fully engaged with that memory, reach out your hand and open the door and invite Jesus in. He wants to come in. He died to come in. I don't have any idea what He will say or do, nor does any one else; we are not God. After you see what is in that memory room you can hold on to it, or you can make a fist, grab hold of it, and make a physical, symbolic act of pulling it out. Stretch out your arm and open your hand giving it away, releasing it to Jesus.

Freedom is knocking at your door. All you have to do is open the door, look at what is in there and give the trash away. You have a choice.

Summary

1. Relationships were designed to fail for those who try to have them without letting God heal their bruises.

2. After one turns twenty, as far as God is concerned, the blame game and finger-pointing days are over. We are responsible for our own actions to Him and others. He is not interested in listening to us blaming Daddy, Mother, and others, no matter how deeply they bruised us (Numbers 14:29).

3. *Grace* is that God loves us no matter what we have done or are doing. *Faith* is when we decide to love Him back. If we truly love Him, then the things we are doing will change. Faith without works is dead.

4. The first step is we have to take is to break out of our prisons, knock down our walls, or take the shields off and be willing to forgive the ones who bruised us, and take responsibility for the ones we bruised. We need to see that our shields or bandages are trash that only isolates us from God and others. We must trust Him to heal and protect us.

5. Then we have to invite Jesus in so that He can talk to us and bring truth and healing.

6. God created something good in everyone. In all my relationships, I could see something really good in the ladies I was with, yet I could not really embrace any of them. I now

know God created something good in all of us. He is the only one who can set each good person free. I am no longer fooling myself that real love was taking place during those passionate moments when our bodies joined. We were just going through the motions without true togetherness. Togetherness and real love takes place only where there is a true commitment and healing.

7. Only free people can embrace each other. Without being free, you cannot pass on peace, and if we are not passing on peace, what are we passing on? Emotionally bruising and scarring those we claim to love is not what God has in mind for us.

8. Only to the extent we are healed and are truly free can we pass on peace and love. Until we go to God and get our hearts right, His blood (power) can't flow through us.

9. It is time for most leaders who call themselves Christians to quit blaming the people for not bringing others to Christ. It is time for the people who attend churches to quit blaming those who don't come to their churches, claiming that these other people just don't want Jesus. It isn't that they don't want Jesus; they are not accepting the Jesus represented by most groups that call themselves Christians. Most churchgoers are not catching fish (people) to bring onto the boat because they are fishing with the wrong bait. It is time we find the Jesus who heals us, get ourselves healed, and bring His healing to the world (Exodus 15:26). If we are not gathering with Jesus and on His side, we are scattering (Matthew 12:30). If we are scattering, whom are we representing? Certainly not God; it would have to be Satan. If we give money to support a group of people who scatter, are we not supporting Satan's kingdom?

Now we need to focus on the promise of freedom and rest. Trust God to help us face the bruises in our lives with the help of others who are headed in the same direction, including individuals and small groups. We are all part of a family of those who have real faith in God. Let us go face the giants, get what God promised, and share it with others. We need each other, and we need leaders like Caleb, who believe the Lord gives victory to those who are not afraid of giants and who know that the grumblers must be left behind (Numbers 13:30). We, as leaders, need to be careful that the grumblers are not grumbling because they have not yet seen the Promised Land in us. They may actually be trying to maintain and reflect peace where there is no peace. Remember, leaders are not just preachers; parents are leaders too, and truthfully, we are all leading someone to heaven or hell at any given time. We are all leading someone to peace or confusion!

Members of God's real church help each other heal from their bruises, rather than just try to comfort their pain. These individuals share about how God has healed them of their bruises, and they let others know they are available to help. That is the real church. That is the road to successful relationships.

God's design for the family is for the father to find peace in and through Him. Only then can the mother lay her head on his chest and experience that peace. Only then can the children experience that peace. Without this structure in place, confusion is the only thing present in the family and passed on to the children. No matter how good you or society may think it looks, it is confusion.

*Note: The single mother's children still have to deal with the father, and the single father's children still have to deal with the mother. The widow may be the exception.

What are you going to do? Are you going to seek the peacemaker or are you going to continue your and your family's journey of confusion?

Billy Burnette   www.stepstohealingamerica.com

Fulfilling Jesus' Commission on Earth: Bible Study

Luke 4:19 explains God the Father's primary mission for Jesus on earth, which is now our primary mission: to bring salvation (freedom) to others and ourselves on earth that will continue when we die and go to heaven.

In Matthew 11:28, Jesus says, "Come to Me, all you who labor and are heavy-laden and overburdened, and I will cause you to rest. [I will ease and relieve and refresh your souls.]"

In Luke 4:18, Jesus says, "The Spirit of the Lord [is] upon Me, because He has anointed Me [the Anointed One, the Messiah] to *preach* the good news (the Gospel) to the *poor*" (emphasis added).

What is the gospel (good news)?

_____

_____

Who are the poor?

_____

_____

Luke 4:19 also says, "He sent me to *announce release* to the captives," or in the King James Version, "He sent me to *heal the brokenhearted,* to preach *deliverance* to the captives" (emphasis added).

Were the broken-hearted actually healed through Jesus? *Yes* or *No*

Were the captives actually set free through Jesus? *Yes* or *No*

How has your broken heart been healed?

_____

Luke 4:19 explains that part of Jesus' and our mission is to give "recovery of sight to the blind."

Are we to see people and things differently? *Yes* or *No*

Has the way you see people changed since you accepted Jesus? If so, how?

_____

_____

_____

_____

_____

Has the way you see yourself changed? If so, how?

_____

_____

_____

_____

_____

Luke 4:19 also says Jesus' and our mission is "to send forth as delivered those who are oppressed [who are downtrodden, bruised, crushed, and broken down by calamity]."

Does this mean He will deliver those who are oppressed? *Yes* or *No*

How have you been set free (delivered) from a calamity in your life?

_____

_____

_____

_____

Isn't this the good news (the gospel) Jesus was sent to preach? He was not only to preach the good news; He was to demonstrate the good news.

After all, Jesus didn't come to tell us how to live. He came to show us how to live, to set us free so we could live ourselves. The law doesn't heal; the blood of Jesus does. Preaching and teaching without the demonstration of inner healing misrepresents Jesus.

Luke 4:19 looks forward to the time when "the accepted and acceptable year of the Lord" will "be proclaimed [the day when salvation and the free favors of God profusely abound]."

Did Jesus just preach the gospel (good news) without the good news being demonstrated? _Yes_ or _No_

Is the demonstration of the gospel happening through your spiritual leaders, or are they just preaching and teaching?

_____

Are you an instrument of freedom and the healing power of God? _Yes_ or _No_

Without the free favors of the gospel abounding in our lives, will people come to know the real Jesus? _Yes_ or _No_

Why are we not doing the things Jesus did through the power of the Holy Spirit?

_____

_____

_____

_____

Jesus said, "I assure you, most solemnly I tell you, if anyone steadfastly believes in Me, he will himself be able to do the things that I do; and he will do even greater things than these, because I go to the Father" (John 14:12).

"Jesus answered them, I have told you so, yet you do not believe me [you do not trust me and rely on Me]. The very works that I do by the power of My Father and in My Father's name bear witness concerning Me [they are My credentials and evidence in support of Me]" (John 10:25).

If the very works Jesus did are not happening through us, where are our credentials that we come from God?

_____

_____

_____

_____

Jesus said, "Take my yoke upon you and learn of Me, for I am gentle (meek) and humble (lowly) in heart, and you will find rest (relief and ease and refreshment and recreation and blessed quiet) for your souls" (Matthew 11:29).

Is there any way other to get to know Jesus other than walking yoked (linked) to Him? *Yes* or *No*

Can you walk that close to Him and not know His voice? *Yes* or *No*

Can you be yoked to Him and not do the things He did? *Yes* or *No*

Simon Peter and his crew fished "all night [exhaustingly] and caught nothing" (Luke 5:5). Jesus had told them, "put out into the deep [water], and lower your nets for a haul" (Luke 5:4). When they obeyed, they caught so many fish that their nets were at the point of breaking. They had to call their partners in another boat to help with the catch.

If you are frustrated with not catching people for the kingdom of God, don't you think Jesus will tell you where to fish for a haul? *Yes* or *No*

Jesus said, "the harvest is plentiful, but the laborers are few" (Matthew 9:37).

Can you believe in Jesus as your Lord and Savior and not be a laborer in His harvest? *Yes* or *No*

Jesus told His disciples to put their nets in the deep water for a haul, which sounds a lot like dealing with the deep issues in our lives and others' lives. Healing the broken-hearted and delivering those who are oppressed are other ways of fishing in the deep waters.

If you are not catching people for the kingdom, do you think it is time to deal with deep issues and listen where Jesus says to fish? *Yes* or *No*

In Matthew 12:30, Jesus says, "He who is not with me [definitely on My side] is against Me, and he who does not [definitely] gather with Me and for My side scatters." We are one of the other.

Can one be yoked to Jesus and not be gathering with Him? *Yes* or *No*

Can one be gathering with Him and not be part of bringing in the harvest? *Yes* or *No*

Are those who are not definitely gathering with Him scattering? *Yes* or *No*

Are those who scatter *for* Jesus or *against* Him? *For* or *Against*

God's intention was that our leaders should equip us to do the work of ministering and building up Christ's body. Jesus was more than a preacher and teacher; He was a trainer (Ephesians 4:13). He told us to go make disciples "of all the nations" (Matthew 28:19–20). He told us that the older men should treat the younger men as brothers (1 Timothy 5:1).

If you are an older Christian man, name the younger men whom you are making disciples.

---

1 Timothy 5:2 says that older women should treat younger women like sisters.

If you are an older Christian woman, name the younger women whom you are making disciples.

If you are not making others into disciples, has anyone ever helped you become a disciple? It is never too late.

Out of Egypt: Bible Study

1. Why did God send Moses to deliver His people? Because they were cr_____ out and He was concerned about their su_____(Exodus 3:7).

2. Did Moses question God? *Yes* or *No* (Exodus 3:11)

3. Did God tell Moses what to do and what to expect would happen when he got to Egypt? *Yes* or *No* (Exodus 3:12–4:14)

4. Who sent Aaron to meet Moses? _____

5. Did God perform miracles through Aaron and Moses to convince the people that God had sent them? *Yes* or *No* (Exodus 4:29)

6. Can magicians perform miracles that duplicate what God has done? *Yes* or *No* (Exodus 7:20–22)

7. What did God do that convinced Pharaoh to let His people go? At midnight, the Lord struck down all the first born in Egypt, from the first born of P_____ to the first born of P_____ and the first born of all the L_____ (Exodus 12:29).

8. Did God warn Moses that He was going to harden Pharaoh's heart and that Pharaoh would come after them? *Yes* or *No* (Exodus 14:1–4)

9. Pharaoh and his officials changed their minds because they realized they had lost their s_____(Exodus 14:5).

10. Why did God harden Pharaoh's heart to come after His people? To gain glory for "My _____" (Exodus 14:4).

11. After all the miracles God had done, they still didn't trust God and got upset with Moses for helping them to gain their freedom. They said, "Didn't we tell you to leave us alone and let us serve the Egyptians?" Did God rescue them? *Yes* or *No* (Exodus 14:10–26)

12. Do you think God wants to set you free when you cry out to Him? *Yes* or *No*

13. Do you think Satan wants to set you free from being his servant? *Yes* or *No*

14. Do you think God is going to come after you after you leave Him? *Yes* or *No*

15. Do you think God has a plan of escape for you? *Yes* or *No*

It is time for us to go fishing and time for us to definitely gather with Him on His side. If you are not gathering and are frustrated, find a deep-water fisherman and let him or her train you on how to fish and how to make disciples of other fish.

You might want to consider the following to pray more effectively when praying for yourself and others.

1. God is God and we are not.

2. Philippians 4:6 says, "Do not fret or have any anxiety about anything, but in every circumstance and in everything, by prayer and petition (definite requests). With thanksgiving, continue to make your wants known to God." We need to listen to God and what He has to say about the request, just as Joshua did when he faced Jericho.

3. 2 Chronicles 7:14 says, "seek, crave, and require of necessity My face." Revelation 3:20 says, "I stand at the door and knock; if anyone hears and listens to and heeds My voice and opens the door, I will come in to Him and will eat with him, and he [will eat] with me." We not only have to make a request; we have to invite Jesus in.

4. John 14:17 says, "And you will know the Truth, and the Truth will set you free." Jesus is the only one who knows the truth about any situation. Once the person hears the truth from Him, the spirits and lies have no more legal right, so that their strength to hang on is gone.

5. Concentrate your prayers on Jesus' goal for you and others. To release you from the things that have you captive, recover your sight so you can see people and circumstances through His eyes, and deliver those who are oppressed [who are downtrodden, bruised, crushed, and broken down by calamity]. So that the accepted and acceptable year of the Lord [the day when salvation and the free favors of God profusely abound. (Luke 4:18,19).

6. People don't have to be Christians to be healed and set free. How many of the people Jesus and the disciples prayed for who were healed and set free were Christians? Jesus wants to demonstrate who He is, so they will know Him and what He can do, so they will accept Him as their Lord and Savior. No one wants to accept someone to be the center of their world that they do not have a personal relationship with and cannot demonstrate who they are.

7. Not everyone who is healed and set free will become Christian; do not get discouraged if they don't. Luke 17 says ten lepers were healed and only one come back to thank Him. You numbers may not be any better, but like Jesus, don't stop praying for those who cry out and those the Holy Spirit leads you to.

8. Remember, the first step is to invite Jesus in and the Holy Spirit, our "comforter (Counselor, Helper, Intercessor, Advocate, Strengthener, Standby)" (John 14:26) will be there to strengthen us and guide us.

9. Ephesians 2:6 says, "He raised us up together with Him and made us sit down together [giving us join seating with Him] in the heavenly sphere [by virtue of our being] in Christ (the Messiah, the Anointed One). We have been given the power; all we have to do is ask what we should say and do, and the power of heaven backs us up.

Conception-to-Birth Prayer

This prayer lets people know God was there even when they were conceived. If the person you are going to pray for will agree to go through this prayer, they will actually experience Jesus. Then they will be a lot more willing to open the door and let Jesus deal with other areas in their lives.

Points of Emphasis

Significant wounding of a person can occur while they are in the mother's womb. During the nine months in utero, many things can happen to a person that can affect their life from that point forward. For this reason, praying for healing for anything that may have occurred in a person's life during this time of conception to birth is a **very important** aspect of inner healing (your salvation).

Outline—The importance of praying about the conception-to-birth period

    A. Conception inconvenient for parents

        1. Parents not married

        2. Baby not planned

        3. Husband away from home

        4. Couple not ready for parenthood

        5. Baby given up for adoption

B.   Conception a result of rape, lust, adultery

   1.   One or both parents under the influence of drugs, alcohol

   2.   Mother possibly a prostitute

   3.   Father a sex addict

C.   Baby unwanted by one or both parents

D.   Parents had to get married because of conception

E.   Mother experienced previous miscarriage or even abortion

   1.   Early trauma by mother invited spirit of fear in

F.   Fear in mother during pregnancy.

G.   Mother's poor self-image during pregnancy

   1.   Possible abuse to mother (parents or partner)

   2.   Possible abuse to/attempted abortion of baby

H.   Sickness, accident, or grieving during pregnancy

I.   Marital discord (one or both parents being unfaithful with others)

J.   Disappointment in sex of baby

K.   Negative, damaging words spoken over baby in utero

L.   Traumatic birth

   1.   Long, hard labor

   2.   Breech birth

Instructions:

1.   Go slowly through each month of the birth process.

2.   Instruct the person you are praying for to nod their head when they have meditated on the words and Scriptures and let them soak in for that month.

3. Have them share with you anything that is going on during that month.

4. Relax. Jesus will show up and take away all their fears and pain. He died to show up.

5. At the end of the ninth month, let the person stay in the presence of Jesus as long as they will. Do not say a word; it is their special time with the Lord. Do not break in on the Lord's conversation. This may be the first time they have experienced the presence of the Lord and the peace that passes all understanding.

Scriptures for Use in Prayer for Conception-to-Birth

Conception
First Month

Hear Him call your name. You were chosen before the foundation of the world! *The Lord has called me from the womb; from the body of my mother He has named my name (Isaiah 49:1b).*

Formation of your body. *For You did form my inward parts; You did knit me together in my mother's womb (Psalm 139).*

Second Month

By the end of this month, it was evident which sex you were. There is nothing you can do to gain God's approval; He has already approved of you and your sexual identity from the very beginning. *"Before I formed you in the womb I knew (and) approved of you (as My chosen instrument), and before you were born" (Jeremiah 1:5a). Thus says the Lord, Who made you and formed you from the womb, Who will help you; Fear not (Isaiah 44:2a).* At the fiftieth day, you changed from embryo to fetus.

Third Month

You are a human being—created by God. *I will confess and praise You for You are fearful and wonderful and for the awful wonder of my birth (Psalm 139:14a).*

Fourth Month

Your mother felt your movement for the first time. The old-fashioned word was "quickened." *In the presence of God, who preserves alive all living things (1 Timothy 6:13a).*

Fifth Month

Claim healing of emotions for you and your mother. *Ask a person if they are feeling any emotions. There is no fear in love (dread does not exist), but full-grown (complete, perfect) love turns fear out of doors and expels every trace of terror! (1John 4:18a).* Mother begins to show. Thank God for your mother, for life and nourishment through her. All internal organs except lungs are fully developed.

Sixth Month

Blessed (happy, to be envied) is (he or she) who believed that there would be a fulfillment of the things that were spoken to (you) from the Lord (Luke 1:45).

Do you believe what the Lord has spoken to you about you? (Give them a chance to nod their head yes or no.)

Seventh Month

Hidden from the world, but not from God. All parts of your body were complete this month. Hearing complete, eyes opened, lungs developed, blood changed to carry oxygen. *My frame was not hidden from You when I was being formed in secret (and) intricately and curiously wrought (as embroiled with various colors) in the earth (a region of darkness and mystery). Your eyes saw my unformed substance, and in Your book all the days (of my life) were written before they ever took shape, when as yet there was none of them. (Psalm 139:15, 16)*

Eighth Month

You and your mother are psychologically connected. You're growing fast, and things are getting a bit crowded. Plans are being made for your arrival. *For thus says the Lord: Behold, I will extend peace to her like a river, and the glory of the nations like an overflowing stream; then you will be nursed, you will be carried on her hip and trotted (lovingly bounced up and down) on her (God's maternal) knees. As a mother comforts, so I will comfort you (Isaiah*

66:12, 13). As you know not what is the way of the wind, or how the spirit comes to the bones in the womb of a pregnant woman, even so you know not the work of God, who does all (Ecclesiastes 11:5).

Ninth Month

Fullness of time—normally 280 days until birth. You are ready to be born. Jesus is there to help deliver you. Jesus said, *"A woman, when she gives birth to a child, has grief (anguish, agony) because her time has come. But when she has delivered the child, she no longer remembers her pain (trouble, anguish) because she is so glad that a (a child, a human being) has been born into the world (John 16:21). Yet You are He Who took me out of the womb; You made me hope and trust when I was on my mother's breast. I was cast upon you from my very birth; from my mother's womb You have been my God (Psalm 22:9, 10). But when God, who had set me apart [even] before I was born and had call me by His grace (His undeserved favor and blessing), saw fit and was pleased (Galatians 1:15).*

Jesus was there to deliver you; you were bonded to Him. Look into His loving eyes and feel His love for you. Do not rush them; let them stay in the presence of Jesus just as long as they want to. Just keep quiet until they open their eyes and want to share with you. Sometimes that will take a long time because they have never rested in the arms of Jesus in their lives.

Praying for Someone Who Has Been Sexually Molested

1. Most people who have been molested blame themselves and Jesus for letting it happen. They have said, *Jesus, if you are so good, why did you let this happen to me?* That is a good question and deserves an answer.

2. They are full of shame and guilt.

3. Have them explain what happened, that is, bringing it into the light. Do not let them go into a lot of detail. If someone wants to go into a lot of detail, they may be in love with their pain and you must ask them, do they just want to talk about their pain or do they want to get rid of it and quit contaminating their family? In other words, do they love their pity parties more than their families? More people are in love with their pain and self-righteousness than you can imagine.

4. We do not know whose fault it was. If it was not their fault, the only person they are going to accept that truth from is Jesus. Give up on your preaching. If it was their fault, only Jesus can forgive them, and He wants to. Let Jesus do the talking without you interfering.

5. Ask the person to go back to the pain, that is, take it to the cross. When a person goes back in their memory and is

brought out from the place where they have tried to bury it, they will feel the pain all over again.

6. After they are there at the cross, instruct them to reach out their hand as if they are opening a doorknob, and invite Jesus in. Jesus will come in, and what He is going to do or say we do not know. We should not try to put words in their mouth.

7. After they are there for a while, ask them to put their hand on their stomach and grab those spirits by closing their hand. Then with the spirits in their still-closed hand, ask Jesus to wash them in His blood and send them back to the molester. Then ask Jesus to go get what they stole from them wash it in His blood and bring it back and place it in their hand. When that part of them that has been stolen comes back in their hand, put their open hand on their stomach and they will be made whole again.

8. After this is over, have them ask God to forgiveness for all the people they have hurt out of their pain. Amen.

9. For most of us, the hardest thing is going to be keeping our mouth shut and letting Jesus do the talking.

Prayer for a Mate of Someone Who Has Been Molested

The spirit of the one who molested your mate has now come into you through your sexual union.

1. Go through the conception-to-birth prayer.

2. Acknowledge that the feelings you have had toward your mate were wrong. You should have been angry at the spirit, not your mate.

3. Ask for forgiveness.

4. Ask the person to go back to the deepest pain they have ever felt from the mate.

5. After they are there and feel all the anger and rejection, they have taken it to the cross.

6. Reach out their hand and invite Jesus in to talk with them.

7. When they are with Jesus, have them put their hand on their stomach and grab the spirit, and with hand closed, reach out their arm and release the Spirit to Jesus to take care of it.

8. Ask them to go back to the anger and rejection and see if there is peace there. If not, repeat the prayer.

Prayer for Older Children of a Parent Who Has Been Sexually Molested

1. It is confession time from the parent. Tell the child what happened to you. Do not go into details. Ask the child to forgive you for the pain and hurt you have passed on to them out of your pain.

2. Go to step 4 of the prayer for the mate and go forward through step 8.

Prayer for Younger Children of a Parent Who Has Been Sexually Molested

1. Tell the child you were hurt when you were young.

2. A spiritual person commands the spirit to come out of the child.

Prayer for Sexual Cleansing

1. The person should go through the Conception-to-Birth prayer first.

2. If there has been a molestation or rape involved, take care of that first.

3. The person has to acknowledge how their sexual relations have ruined and will continue relationships. Repent.

4. Close their eyes and go back to their most memorable sexual experience and invite Jesus in.

After Jesus speaks to them, have them grab their stomach and hold all the spirits of the ones planted in them through sexual relations.